Relativism

Central Problems of Philosophy
Series Editor: John Shand

This series of books presents concise, clear, and rigorous analyses of the core problems that preoccupy philosophers across all approaches to the discipline. Each book encapsulates the essential arguments and debates, providing an authoritative guide to the subject while also introducing original perspectives. This series of books by an international team of authors aims to cover those fundamental topics that, taken together, constitute the full breadth of philosophy.

Published titles

Free Will
Graham McFee

Universals
J. P. Moreland

Knowledge
Michael Welbourne

Forthcoming titles

Action
Rowland Stout

Paradox
Doris Olin

Analysis
Michael Beaney

Perception
Barry Maund

Artificial Intelligence
Matthew Elton & Michael Wheeler

Rights
Jonathan Gorman

Causation and Explanation
Stathis Psillos

Scepticism
Neil Gascoigne

Meaning
David Cooper

Self
Stephen Burwood

Mind and Body
Robert Kirk

Truth
Pascal Engel

Modality
Joseph Melia

Value
Chris Cherry

Ontology
Dale Jacquette

Relativism

Paul O'Grady

McGill-Queen's University Press
Montreal & Kingston • Ithaca

© Paul O'Grady 2002

ISBN   0-7735-2379-0 (bound)
ISBN   0-7735-2380-4 (paper)

Published simultaneously outside North America
by Acumen Publishing Limited

McGill-Queen's University Press acknowledges the financial support of
the Government of Canada through the Book Publishing Development
Program (BPIDP) for its activities.

National Library of Canada Cataloguing in Publication Data

O'Grady, Paul, 1964-
         Relativism / Paul O'Grady.

(Central problems of philosophy)
Includes bibliographical references and index.
ISBN 0-7735-2379-0 (bound).—ISBN 0-7735-2380-4 (pbk.)

         1. Relativity. I. Title. II. Series.

BD221.O37 2002   121   C2002-902383-1

Designed and typeset by Kate Williams, Abergavenny.
Printed and bound by Biddles Ltd., Guildford and King's Lynn.

For Gabrielle

Contents

Preface

Philosophy is an abstract and theoretical discipline. Because of this, many outside it (and not a few within it) think that it has little impact on the everyday life of people. This has been especially accented in recent years, as increasing standards of professionalization mean that philosophers tend to write explicitly just for others in their field and leave the general public in the dark. Nevertheless, philosophy has always had an impact on human culture, shaping currents and tendencies, supplying ideologies, vocabularies and concepts and offering ideals that penetrate to all aspects of society. For example, the works of Aristotle and Aquinas influenced a great number of people over many centuries through the mediation of the Catholic Church. The dialectics of Hegel, turned on their head by Marx, reached a multitude through various socialist movements. The existentialists' analysis of nihilism, meaninglessness and boredom pervaded the literature and cinematic culture of the twentieth century. But what sort of impact could the work of contemporary analytical philosophy have, when at least one critic has noted, "Linguistic philosophy corrupts no one. What it does do is bore them" (Gellner 1959: 218)? Now this is unfair, because the levels of abstraction and sophistication found in analytical philosophy can be found in most of the works of the great philosophers. While it may not immediately seem clear how such technical work might have cultural repercussions, history shows that material just as abstruse has had such an effect. Recent philosophical investigations of relativism seem to be a case in point.

One of the effects of the general acceleration of life in the modern period is that ideas are disseminated more quickly and their effects seen more rapidly than in previous times. Abstract philosophical theory affects general culture more rapidly. Terms coined just a decade or two earlier have now become common coinage. For example, the general characterization of the present era as that of postmodernity derives from highly speculative and theoretical work in continental philosophy, but one finds it nowadays as a given in newspapers, television and the arts. One of the pervasive features of postmodernism has been an acceptance of relativism: there are no longer any absolutes, foundations are gone, and the task of the intellectual is now to adapt and show others how to adapt to this shifting milieu.

This attitude can be found across a great number of the social sciences and the humanities. The famous hoax perpetrated by the physicist Alan Sokal, who published a spoof paper entitled "Transgressing the Boundaries: Towards a Transformative Hermeneutics of Quantum Gravity", was an attempt to draw attention to the uncritical pervasiveness of relativistic thinking (see Sokal & Bricmont 1998). The "Sokal affair" provoked fierce discussion, where relativists traded blows with crusading anti-relativists. Extremists on both sides tended to polarize the discussion. Yet there still is a general acceptance that relativism of some form is the new orthodoxy among those who are theoretically attuned in the humanities, whereas bluff assertion of reality is the mode of those closer to the laboratory bench. Terms originally deriving from philosophers, such as "paradigm", "language-game", "worldview" and "conceptual scheme", are used to reinforce the relativist view. Some of the responses to this relativism are extreme withdrawals to kinds of fundamentalism, whether religious, political or scientistic. In all of this one can see the impact of philosophical thought in society.

This book is an attempt to examine relativism and evaluate the philosophical case for it. It carries this out within a particular philosophical tradition, namely the analytic tradition. The incredible diversity and proliferation of relativistic ideas necessitates making choices on what to cover and how to deal with it. I will not deal with authors from the continental tradition, but hope that readers familiar with that material will find the analyses here helpful in understanding the issues treated by those thinkers. Neither will I deal with ideas associated with Einstein and relativity theory in physics because, by and large, they have had little enough effect on the philosophical discussion. What I will do is distinguish different kinds of relativism, discussing and evaluating them in a topic-based way. Given that relativism is such an important facet of contemporary intellectual life, this book provides a way into that material, charting a path and defending a particular reading of the topic.

Many people helped in the writing of this book, whether by conversation or by more detailed written comments. Thanks to Lilian Alweiss, David Berman, Martin Cogan, Anthony Cullen, Anthony Dardis, Alan Forde, Brian Garvey, Richard Gray, Jeff Kallen, Jim Levine, Bill Lyons, Robert McKim, Vasilis Politis, Oran Ryan, John Shand, Alan Weir and two anonymous readers. Thanks also to the students who participated in the Senior Sophister seminars at Trinity College Dublin, who were the guinea pigs for earlier versions of this material. I am grateful for two grants from my college: one for replacement teaching during sabbatical leave in Michaelmas Term 2001 and the other from the Provost's Academic Development Fund.

Paul O'Grady
Trinity College Dublin

1 Introduction to relativism

Relativism in contemporary thought

Looking back a century, one can see a striking degree of homogeneity among the philosophers of the early twentieth century in terms of the topics central to their concerns. More striking still is the apparent obscurity and abstruseness of those concerns, which seem at first glance to be far removed from the great debates of previous centuries, between realists and idealists, say, or rationalists and empiricists.

The German philosopher Gottlob Frege (1848–1925) devoted his career to the foundations of mathematics and was rewarded with profound indifference from his fellow philosophers and mathematicians. The English philosopher Bertrand Russell (1872–1970) devoted his early work to exactly the same issue, culminating in *Principia Mathematica*, which was such an intellectual effort, he said, that it rendered him incapable of ever producing such detailed work again. In his early work the Austrian philosopher Ludwig Wittgenstein (1889–1951) focused even more narrowly on a critique of the work of Frege and Russell on the meaning of the logical constants. He also became aware of how much could be gained from such minute examination, saying that his work had widened out from the foundations of logic to the nature of the world. The Austrian philosopher Edmund Husserl (1859–1938) also started with the philosophy of geometry, before developing the phenomenological method, which was geared toward answering questions emerging from his earlier work. On the other side of the Atlantic, C. S. Peirce (1839–1914), the founder of American pragmatism, had been concerned with the nature of language and how it related to thought. From this he developed his theory of semiotics as a method for philosophy.

From these initial concerns came some of the great themes of twentieth-century philosophy. How exactly does language relate to thought? Can there be complex, conceptual thought without language? Are there irredeemable problems about putative private thought? These issues are captured under the general label the "Linguistic Turn". The subsequent development of those early-twentieth-century positions has led to a bewildering heterogeneity in philosophy in the early twenty-first century. The very nature of philosophy is itself radically disputed: "analytic", "continental", "postmodern", "critical theory", "feminist" and "non-Western" are all prefixes that give a different meaning when joined to "philosophy". The variety of thriving different schools, the number of professional philosophers, the proliferation of publications, the development of technology in helping research (word-processing, databases, the Internet, and so on) all manifest a radically different situation to that of one hundred years ago.

Nevertheless, in the midst of all this bustling diversity one can detect some common themes, one of which derives directly from the Linguistic Turn. The move to making language the centre of philosophical concern meant taking into account the social context in which language is produced. A unifying characteristic of much late-twentieth-century philosophy is attention to the social nature of thought, and so to the social dimension to our theories about reality. One might say that the Social Turn is as defining a characteristic of contemporary philosophy as the Linguistic Turn had been of the earlier period. Consider a representative list of some of the most prominent contemporary philosophers: Brandom, Davidson, Derrida, Habermas, McDowell, Putnam, Rorty. They all explicitly refer to societal forces operating on our thinking and attempt to draw out the implications for questions about meaning, ontology, truth and knowledge. Needless to say, they have quite different takes on what those implications are.

One such implication, which many have drawn, is that truth, meaning, ontology and knowledge are no longer best regarded as stable, unified concepts. In so far as there are many different societies, many different points of view, there is no single defining view that fixes the truth about any of these issues. Attempts to do so are often branded as cultural or intellectual imperialism – typically the imperialism of western middle-class men. Those who endorse such a critique typically view philosophy itself as inextricably tied up with these imperialistic tendencies and strike out in a new direction, eschewing philosophy in favour of critical theory, postmodernism, feminism, gender theory or whatever. This is not to say that those areas are necessarily outside philosophy, but that the more radical proponents of them want to move beyond contemporary philosophy.

Those remaining, however uneasily, within what can be regarded as academic philosophy are more worried about the diversity of approaches, and this is where the issue of relativism arises quite sharply. Relativism is nearly universally regarded as a bogeyman. Hardly any philosopher wants to be called a relativist; nearly everyone is against it – whatever it is. Even those who are regarded by their fellow philosophers as archetypal relativists vigorously deny that they are relativists and indeed launch strong attacks on what they see as relativism. So Rorty says, "'Relativism' is the view that every belief on a certain topic, or perhaps about any topic, is as good as every other. No one holds this view" (1982: 166). Putnam says, "That (total) relativism is inconsistent is a truism among philosophers ... The plethora of relativistic doctrines being marketed today (and marketed by highly intelligent thinkers) indicated [that] simple refutation will not suffice" (1981: 119). Yet when Michael Devitt argues against relativism in his book *Realism and Truth* he says, "Putnam's position is reminiscent of the relativistic Kantianism I attributed to Kuhn, Feyerabend and the radical philosophers of science" (1997: 230). In his chapter on Rorty he says, "There are certainly plenty of signs of epistemic relativism in Rorty" (1997: 205). And this assessment could be repeated again and again among contemporary philosophers who regard Rorty and Putnam as being paradigmatically relativistic thinkers.

Whatever else one might take from the quotations just given, it is clear that "relativism" means a multitude of different things and that adding the title to any position usually means inviting a barrage of criticism from even those who are supposed to be on your side. In a recent discussion of the topic, Susan Haack sets up a bewildering variety of "relativisms" (1998: 149). She suggests that one could build up an identikit picture of the family using the following schema:

... IS RELATIVE TO ...

(1) meaning	(a) language
(2) reference	(b) conceptual scheme
(3) truth	(c) theory
(4) metaphysical commitment	(d) scientific paradigm
(5) ontology	(e) version, depiction, description
(6) reality	(f) culture
(7) epistemic values	(g) community
(8) moral values	(h) individual
(9) aesthetic values	•
•	•
•	•

Not every item on the left could fit with every one on the right and vice versa but, among the ones that can be linked, the sense of a large, loosely connected family begins to emerge. This illustrates starkly a grave problem with discussions of "relativism": the multiplicity of positions covered by the term. Attacks on it, and indeed defences of it, usually confuse a variety of importantly different positions under a single label.

So what do I mean by "relativism"? I'll begin by jettisoning some issues. I will not deal with moral relativism. This is the view that there are no universal moral norms – that morality is local or culturally relative or some other non-universal view. A great deal of literature exists on this, but I shall pass over it simply because it is not the focus of this book. The kind of relativism I'm interested in exploring could perhaps be called "cognitive relativism". A simple way of characterizing this is that it is all the relativism that's left when you leave out moral and aesthetic relativism. It covers issues in epistemology, metaphysics, philosophy of language and philosophy of logic, among others. However, in leaving aside moral relativism I am not ignoring the view that values have a role to play in cognitive relativism – an issue I shall discuss below. Relativism is also sometimes confused with scepticism. I'll discuss this in some detail in Chapter 4. Briefly, cognitive relativism rejects some of the assumptions held by sceptics and so rejects scepticism itself, making space for legitimate, fallible, alternative conceptions of reality.

On a question of terminology, relativism is generally contrasted with its polar opposite: absolutism. Calling something relative is to say that it arises from or is determined by something else; it is dependent on its relation to some other thing. Something absolute is independent and doesn't require relationship to anything else. However, this is a very general and not very informative characterization. The sorts of dependence and independence in question may be of very different kinds. I shall examine in more detail specific forms of cognitive relativism in this chapter in "The cognitive relativism family" (pp. 19–24), which will serve to make more concrete what is involved. However, the point I want to make here is that the terms "relative" and "absolute" will be used thoughout the rest of the book as opposed terms. So anti-relativists will be characterized as absolutists.

Another term sometimes used instead of relativism is "pluralism". This characterizes the situation where there are alternatives – where there is more than one canonical or valid account of reality. As will become clearer in the remainder of the book, I hold that some forms of relativism are rationally acceptable, and others are not. The term "pluralism" may be taken as synonymous with those forms of relativism that are acceptable and I will not dwell any further on this essentially terminological issue. But now, before presenting different kinds of cognitive relativism, I will examine some key positions in twentieth-century philosophy that paved the way for relativistic thinking.

Sources of contemporary relativism

A distinctive feature of twentieth-century philosophy has been a series of sustained challenges to dualisms that were taken for granted in earlier periods. The split between mind and body that dominated most of the modern period was attacked in a variety of different ways by twentieth-century thinkers. Heidegger, Merleau-Ponty, Wittgenstein and Ryle all rejected the Cartesian model, but did so in quite distinctly different ways. Other cherished dualisms have also been attacked – for example, the analytic–synthetic distinction, the dichotomy between theory and practice and the fact–value distinction. However, unlike the rejection of Cartesian dualism, these debates are still live, with substantial support for either side.

While a reasonably unified philosophical community existed at the beginning of the twentieth century, by the middle of the century philosophy had split into distinct traditions with little contact between them. Russell, Husserl and James had been aware of each other's work. However, the traditions following on from them tended to operate by and large in ignorance of each other. The English-based tradition of Russell–Wittgenstein–Ryle–Austin and the American-based tradition of James–Lewis–Quine–Putnam did interact with each other, but left alone the Husserl–Heidegger–Sartre–Derrida tradition and were likewise ignored by them. It was only towards the close of the century that a more ecumenical spirit began to arise on both sides. Nevertheless, despite the philosophical Cold War, certain curiously similar tendencies emerged on all sides during the mid-twentieth century, which aided the rise of cognitive relativism as a significant phenomenon. I shall address three of these here.

Rejecting the theory–practice dichotomy

In the ancient world, the metaphysical and ethical parts of philosophy were in closer contact than has been the case subsequently. Questions about how one should live and what is the good life led naturally to abstract reflections on being, knowledge and all the other staples of philosophical reflection. The passion for systematization of the medieval period also made for unified accounts of reality, where ethical considerations and prescriptions for conduct were held to derive from the very fabric of reality. Goodness and being were understood as different facets of the same basic reality. However, in the early modern period this unified approach began to unravel. The investigation of the nature of reality began to pull apart from questions about morality. As technological and scientific advances shed greater light on the mysteries of nature, the problem of human conduct and behaviour came to be seen as a more localized problem, one not connected to discussions of the nature of reality.

While science offered accounts of the laws of nature and the constituents of matter, and revealed the hidden mechanisms behind appearances, a split appeared in the kinds of knowledge available to enquirers. On the one hand there were the objective, reliable, well-grounded results of empirical enquiry into nature, and on the other the subjective, variable and controversial results of enquiries into morals, society, religion and so on. There was the realm of the world, which existed imperiously and massively independent of us, and the human world itself, which was complex, varied and dependent on us. The philosophical conception that developed from this picture was that of a split between a view of reality that is independent of human input and reality dependent on human beings. Bernard Williams has labelled the former the "absolute conception of reality" (1978: 64–8). Genuine knowledge is knowledge of that which is there independently of our knowing of it: knowledge of what is there anyway.

Human knowledge is an effort adequately to capture or represent this reality. While different representations of it are possible, the constant impetus of human enquiry is to try to get to a more inclusive representation that can explain localized differences. Philosophers of the modern period worked within this conception in developing and employing the distinction between primary and secondary qualities. Primary qualities are those aspects of reality that are there independent of human cognition – for example, shape, motion and mass. Secondary qualities require conscious awareness for their existence – for example, colours, sounds and so on. The vibrations in the air that hit my eardrum and lead me to hear the traffic outside are explicable in terms that don't bring in consciousness. However, my hearing the sound requires conscious awareness. So one set of phenomena belong absolutely to the furniture of the world and would be there with no one to know them. Other phenomena are products of human receptivity and consciousness and are therefore dependent on human cognition. These are not part of the absolute conception of reality.

It was thought that philosophy could help the pursuit of the absolute conception of reality first of all by supplying epistemological foundations for it. However, after many failed attempts at this, other philosophers appropriated the more modest task of clarifying the meanings and methods of the primary investigators (the scientists). Philosophy can come into its own when sorting out the more subjective aspects of the human realm: ethics, aesthetics, politics.

However, what is distinctive of the investigation of the absolute conception is its disinterestedness, its cool objectivity, its demonstrable success in achieving results. It is pure theory – the acquisition of a true account of reality. While these results may be put to use in technology, the goal of enquiry is truth itself with no utilitarian end in view. The human striving for knowledge, noted by Aristotle at the beginning of his *Metaphysics*, gets its fullest realization in the scientific effort to flesh out this absolute conception of reality.

This absolute conception of reality came under attack from different quarters in the twentieth century. On a descriptive level, historians and philosophers of science held that it gave a distorted account of how enquiry actually proceeded. Scientists are members of human society just as much as anyone else. They are influenced by fashion, politics, economics, social status, the search for patronage and many other elements from the "subjective" realm. Furthermore, the project of enquiry is not describable in terms of setting out rules and methods, and the histories of the various sciences are littered with stories of chance, intrigue, lucky blunders and wayward genius. So the picture of the scientist as somehow removed from the messy subjective realities of human existence doesn't hold up. Yet one could still claim that, despite its murky history and provenance, science still delivers the pristine goods: the unpolluted absolute conception of reality. The glory of science is its pulling the objective truth from the murk of human interaction with reality. However, this was further challenged by examining very idea of objectivity used in articulating the notion of the absolute conception of reality.

One problem regularly pointed out is that the absolute conception of reality leaves itself open to massive sceptical challenge. If such a pure de-humanized picture of reality is the goal of enquiry, how could we ever reach it? Surely we would inevitably infect it with human subjectivity in our very effort to grasp it. Therefore we are condemning ourselves to the melancholy conclusion that we will never really have knowledge of reality – a sceptical stance. If one wanted to reject such a sceptical conclusion, a rejection of the conception of objectivity underlying it would be required.

A different notion of objectivity rests on the idea of inter-subjectivity. What is objective is that on which reasonable people agree. Unlike in the absolute conception of reality, one doesn't have to claim that there is no human input into the picture of reality acquired in enquiry. Rather, as William James put it, "the trail of the human serpent is thus over everything" (1981: 33). This doesn't render the results of enquiry less objective; it changes our conception of objectivity. We do get in touch with a reality independent of human thought, but mediated via human thought.

How this connects to relativism is that reality can be so mediated in a variety of different ways, which are not reducible to each other. The representations of objective reality may differ depending on the concepts we use to think about it. Different features of reality come to the fore as we deploy different sets of concepts to deal with it. Philosophers from different traditions, such as Wittgenstein, Heidegger and William James, came to hold versions of this view. With such a view, there arises a tension between, on the one hand, a free-for-all approach, where a multiplicity of conflicting views can be accepted with insouciance and, on the other, the drive to limit such proliferation, to exercise some kind of cognitive control on what is acceptable and what is not. We can look a little more closely at some of these ideas in discussing frameworks, below. Meanwhile, this challenge to the sharp dichotomy between theory and practice had the effect of putting another related dichotomy under threat, namely the distinction between facts and values.

Rejecting the fact–value dichotomy

The notion of "fact" is closely tied to that of the absolute conception of reality. Facts are independent, objective, solid, dependable, invariant and reliable. They are to be contrasted with the subjective, mutable and unreliable: emotions, wishes, dreams, delusions and other subjective projections of humankind. One casualty of the dominance of the absolute conception of reality was the notion of value. From its former place as rooted in being, it came to be seen as a kind of projection, a way human beings have of colouring the facts, which exist independently of any such colour. So language can be split into descriptive vocabulary, which articulates the facts, and evaluative vocabulary, which reports our attitude to such facts. Emotivist theories of ethics propose this dichotomy and take the sharp fact–value split as given.

Now on the absolute conception of reality, facts exist independently of human cognition. Nevertheless, in order for human beings to know such facts, they must be conceptualized. We dress the world in concepts in order to think of it. This point is used by those against the absolute conception of reality to challenge it and its associated fact–value dichotomy. The world doesn't automatically conceptualize itself. The story of the development of human knowledge is the story of the creative development of more and more concepts to articulate the way the world is. However, we develop concepts that pick out those features of the world in which we have an interest, and not others. We use concepts that are related to our sensory capacities. For example, we don't have readily available concepts to discriminate colours that are beyond the visible spectrum. No such concepts were available at all prior to our deepening understanding of light, and such concepts as there are now are not widely deployed, since most people don't have reason to use them.

What does that say about "facts"? Well, we can still accept that the world makes facts true or false. However what counts as a fact is partially dependent on human input. One part, just discussed, is the availability of concepts to describe such facts. Another part is the establishing of whether something actually is a fact or not. That is, when we decide that something is a fact, it fits into our body of knowledge of the world. However, for something to have such a role is governed by a number of considerations, all of which are value-laden. We license things as facts that are instrumentally efficacious – that is, which help us make predictions. We accept as facts those things that make theories simple, that allow for greater generalization, that cohere with other facts and so on. The features are not reducible to physical facts themselves on an absolute conception. They are values – elements where human interest enters the picture. Hence in rejecting the view that facts exist independently of human concepts or human epistemology we get to the situation where facts are understood to be dependent on certain kinds of values – the values that govern enquiry in all its multiple forms – scientific, historical, literary, legal and so on.

So does that make facts subjective? No, but it does reinforce the need to reinterpret what is meant by the subjective–objective distinction. Certain features of reality are stable, reliable, dependable and factual. But objective status is not accorded to these features of reality because they are totally independent of human cognition and interest. They are contrasted with those other features of reality that are unreliable, unstable, undependable and non-factual. The difference is not that the latter features are infected by human interests, but that the kinds of values exhibited by what we call "facts" are not present in things that are non-factual: the values of coherence, instrumental adequacy and so on.

Two philosophical pictures are in competition here about the relation of mind to world. The older picture is one in which the world exists totally independently of human construction, and mind merely mirrors it. The more recent picture allows some degree of human creativity in constructing the world in which we live. Adherents of this latter picture leave open the possibility of multiple ways of describing the world. In so far as interests and values may differ, there may be different accounts of the facts in the world. Anti-relativists strive to contain this by emphasizing the limitations on such versions and the possibility of convergence into a large unified picture of reality. Relativists emphasize differences and the non-assimilation of versions of the world to each other. One of the means by which relativists do this is by using the idea that the world is mediated through a structure that yields different accounts of reality to us relative to that structure. Different terms have been used for such a structure – for example, "conceptual scheme", "paradigm", "linguistic framework" and "language game". That our knowledge of the world comes via such a structure is a distinctive element in a number of eminent twentieth-century philosophers' work and a main plank in relativists' thinking.

Framework ideas

The American philosopher C. I. Lewis (1883–1946) was influenced by both Kant's division of knowledge into that which is given and that which processes the given, and pragmatism's emphasis on the relation of thought to action. Fusing both these sources into a distinctive position, Lewis rejected the sharp dichotomies of both theory–practice and fact–value. He conceived of philosophy as the investigation of the categories by which we think about reality. He denied that experience conceptualizes itself: that the way we think about reality is unambiguously determined by that reality itself. The way we think about reality is socially and historically shaped. Concepts, the meanings that are shared by human beings, are a product of human interaction with the world. Theory is infected by practice and facts are shaped by values. Concepts structure our experience and reflect our interests, attitudes and needs. The distinctive role for philosophy, on Lewis's account, is to investigate the criteria of classification and principles of interpretation we use in our multifarious interactions with the world. Specific issues come up for individual sciences, which will be the philosophy of that science. But there are also common issues for all sciences and non-scientific activities, reflection on which is the specific task of philosophy.

In *Mind and the World Order* (1956), Lewis famously developed an epistemology that distinguished different elements in the act of knowledge. He held that the given, that which is immediately available to consciousness, is to be distinguished from the concept by which the given is thought and from the act of interpretation that unites the concept and the given. The investigation of human concepts, their inferential connections and mutual interrelationships is the special task of philosophy. This kind of reflection is not empirical, since that kind of enquiry is scientific. But reflective enquiry across our actions, inferences and systems of classification yields ethics, logic and metaphysics, respectively.

The basic system of classification by which we describe the fundamental nature of reality is, for Lewis, the special province of metaphysics. The categories used by us are not read off, as it were, from reality, but reflect enduring human interests. In that respect reality is relative to a system of concepts. The world as we know it is shaped by the concepts we use to interpret it. Success in our actions and projects is the means by which our concepts are governed by experience. Faulty and useless concepts lead to bad predictions and unsuccessful courses of action.

The framework idea in Lewis is that of the system of categories by which we mediate reality to ourselves: "The problem of metaphysics is the problem of the categories" (Lewis 1956: 10), "Experience doesn't categorize itself" (*ibid*.: 14) and "the categories are ways of dealing with what is given to the mind" (*ibid*.: 31). Such a framework can change across societies and historical periods: "our categories are almost as much a social product as is language, and in something like the same sense" (*ibid*.: 21). Lewis didn't specifically thematize the question that there could be alternative sets of such categories, but he did acknowledge the possibility on occasion.

> This present classification [of a fountain pen] depends on that learned relation of this experience to other experience and to my action, which the shape, size, etc., of this object was not then a sign of. A savage in New Guinea, lacking certain interests and habits of action which are mine, would not so classify it. (Lewis 1956: 49)

Couldn't the world be presented in radically different ways depending on the set of categories used? In so far as the categories interpret reality and there is no unmediated access to reality in itself, the only curbs on systems of categories would be pragmatic ones. These wouldn't necessarily force one to accept just one set of categories, in so far as different circumstances could lead different kinds of categories to be more or less successful. Hence there is the potential for a great deal of relativism in Lewis's work.

Sharing some common sources with Lewis, the German philosopher Rudolf Carnap (1891–1970) articulated a doctrine of linguistic frameworks that was radically relativistic in its implications. Carnap was influenced by the Kantian idea of the constitution of knowledge: that our knowledge is in some sense the end result of a cognitive process. He also shared Lewis's pragmatism and valued the practical application of knowledge. However, as a logical empiricist he was heavily influenced by the developments of modern science, regarding scientific knowledge as the paradigm of knowledge and motivated by a desire to be rid of pseudo-knowledge such as traditional metaphysics and theology. These influences remained constant as his work moved through various distinct stages and when he moved to live in America. In 1950 he published a paper entitled "Empiricism, Semantics and Ontology" in which he articulated his views about linguistic frameworks.

Carnap had a deflationist view of philosophy. That is, he believed that philosophy had no role in telling us truths about reality, but rather played its part in clarifying meanings for scientists. Now some philosophers believed that this clarificatory project itself led to further philosophical investigations and special philosophical truths about meaning, truth, necessity and so on. Carnap rejected this view, believing that it led back to traditional-style philosophy and vacuity. The key problem with such enquiries was that there was no way of resolving them. This was the core contrast with science, where methods of resolution were available and genuine knowledge secured. So Carnap held that philosophy should not seek its own truths, but rather operate as a technical ancillary to science. Questions about meaning, logical implication, criteria for confirmation and so on can be investigated by philosophers. They can build theoretical models for such issues that will be submitted to the actual researchers in these areas and used by them as they apply to actual problems. Carnap himself attempted to work out systems of inductive and modal logic that could be used to aid empirical enquiry and abet research in semantics and mathematical science, but which crucially would not spawn traditional-style questions in metaphysics and epistemology. In this way philosophical problems are "deflated" to practical choices for scientists.

One of his central tools in this project was the notion of a linguistic framework. This is a system of linguistic rules, which license the use of certain terms and legislate for their relationship to other terms. For example, the use of number terms might be introduced in a set of rules, showing how they relate and interact in arithmetic. Relative to this framework, questions about numbers are easily answerable. Carnap calls these kinds of questions "internal questions" and what characterizes them is that they presuppose the existence of such a framework. Likewise, one can have frameworks with rules for speaking about physical objects, properties or the spatiotemporal realm of physics. Relative to the framework, internal questions are uncontroversially answerable. However, philosophical questions arise when one tries to answer questions independent of such a framework. Do numbers *really* exist? Do properties *really* exist? Carnap calls these "external questions", because they are outside the context of a linguistic framework. Such questions are improper, because the choice of framework is pragmatically decided on. If it is useful to speak of numbers, then such a framework will be used; if it is useful to speak of properties, then that framework will be used. The only appropriate external questions are ones about the expediency of using a framework or not. Questions about trying to relate the frameworks to some anterior reality are deflated to the practical question of choice of framework. Such a position gives a very wide range of options and the possibility of a bewildering multiplicity of frameworks and diverse positions. Carnap points to a kind of natural selection process in relation to these frameworks.

> The acceptance or rejection of abstract linguistic forms, just as the acceptance or rejection of any other linguistic forms in any branch of science, will finally be decided by their efficiency as instruments, the ratio of the results achieved to the amount and complexity of the effort required . . . Let us grant to those who work in any special field of investigation the freedom to use any form of expression which seems useful to them; the work in the field will sooner or later lead to the elimination of those forms which have no useful function.   (Carnap 1950: 221)

This intellectual natural selection will nevertheless allow for a great variety, just as biological natural selection does. So Carnap's linguistic frameworks offer much scope for relativistically inclined philosophers.

Ludwig Wittgenstein (1889–1951) is possibly the most important developer of framework ideas of the twentieth century and is famous for producing two influential philosophies. The first, developed in the *Tractatus Logico-Philosophicus* (1961), gives an account of the relationship of language, thought and reality that articulates the essence of language and the picturing relation between language and the fixed nature of reality. His later philosophy, powerfully presented in the posthumous *Philosophical Investigations* (1953), is a sustained critique of many aspects of that first account. He rejects the idea that language has an essence. He espouses a view of philosophy as therapeutic, not advancing theses or holding positions but clarifying language, weaning us away from mythologies embedded in our habitual ways of thinking.

In rejecting the notion that language has a single determinate essence, Wittgenstein proposed to view language as comprising language games. A language game is a complex whole of verbal usage and associated activities. Words don't simply label or stand for objects, but relate to each other and the world in highly complex ways. Words are like tools: there are many different kinds performing many different kinds of activities. Therefore there are many different language games and many different associated forms of life, the kinds of activities associated with the language game. The language games are governed by grammatical rules. Rules of grammar prescribe the modes of representation by which the world is represented to us. For example, we speak about colour in certain ways. Wittgenstein holds that these ways of speaking are not automatically prescribed by reality: colours don't divide themselves up into discrete concepts and lay out how we must think about them. Rules for the use of colour words constitute our habitual ways of speaking about colour. And likewise for many other kinds of thing. Wittgenstein emphasized that it was most important not to conflate one language game with another, or to think that there are super language games that govern all the others.

This view of language as composed of many different autonomous language games, with their own rules of grammar, fits well with relativism. A quite popular use of Wittgenstein's idea was to try to defend religious belief against rationalistic critique by claiming that religion is its own language game and that it is illicit to use criteria from another language game (usually science) to challenge it. So the picture of separate language games of, for example, science, religion, art, politics and feminism became popular among those interested in defending relativism. This is not to say that Wittgenstein himself espoused such views, but his views lent themselves to such use.

Further aspects of Wittgenstein's work aided relativism. He had thought at one stage of using the phrase "I'll teach you differences" as an epigram to the *Philosophical Investigations*. He believed that one of the chief problems in philosophizing was a one-sided diet of examples and a lack of imagination, which tended to keep people stuck in an intellectual rut. To counter this he used examples of odd tribes, aliens and animals to try to confront us with the views of beings who thought in a manner quite different to the way we think. In his final writings on epistemology, *On Certainty*, he spoke of the distinction between beliefs that are fundamental to our thinking and those that are less fundamental and that we are happy to alter. Using the image of a river bed, he held that fundamental ideas may change like the river bed, but at a slower rate than the current of less fundamental ideas. However, he seems to hold that all is mutable and suggests that our knowledge can be viewed as having a framework of basic ideas supporting a superstructure of less basic ones. But the framework may alter and, indeed, there may be alternative frameworks.

The American W. V. Quine (1908–2000) was one of the earliest to popularize the phrase "conceptual scheme" in his writings. Influenced by logical postivism (mainly Carnap) and pragmatism (mainly Dewey), Quine's thought dominated Anglo-American thought in the second half of the twentieth century. Quine thought of knowledge instrumentally: knowledge is a tool we use to deal with the world. It is also culturally constructed: a posit. Quine thinks of the deliverances of science as posits – ways we have of making sense of the world. He thinks that the modern world of physics is superior to that of the Homeric gods, but the superiority is epistemological. Physics and the Homeric gods are conflicting accounts of reality, both construed as posits, but the physics posit has better evidence for it than the Homeric posit.

A conceptual scheme, for Quine, is the framework of assumptions we bring to enquiry. We do not think in a vacuum. Our conceptual scheme is revisable. We alter some beliefs, and hold on to others. However, there is no neutral position, no place of cosmic exile as Quine describes it. To talk about a world is to apply some conceptual scheme to it. Children are inducted into a conceptual scheme as they learn language. Quine thinks of science as a refinement of the conceptual scheme of common sense, speaking of physical objects, identity, reference, abstract objects, etc. Now it is clear that Quine thinks of science, and specifically physics, as having the most inclusive conceptual scheme. It covers everything that exists. This conceptual scheme is the best one we have for understanding the world and for predicting changes in it. It is the most inclusive account we have. However, Quine accepts that there are other ways of talking about the world. Using Wittgenstein's term "language-game", Quine says that there are other kinds of language use, such as fiction and poetry. These present imaginary worlds, alternative takes on this world, new ways of seeing. They use different conceptual schemes. So far so good. But could there be alternative conceptual schemes that are factual – that present radically different factual accounts of reality to the standard ones we have? There are the resources in Quine's philosophy to defend this view. For example, he presented the view that all our beliefs are in principle revisable: none stand absolutely. He held that theory is underdetermined by evidence: there are always alternative possible theories compatible with the same basic evidence. The abandonment of fixed a priori knowledge and the logical space for alternative theories, coupled with the use of the notion of the conceptual scheme, make Quine's work a fertile resource for relativists. Quine's actual position will be discussed in Chapter 3.

Finally, the work of the American historian of science T. S. Kuhn (1922–1996) has greatly helped the proliferation of relativistic ideas. His notion of "paradigm" has had widespread influence beyond the confines of history and philosophy of science. A paradigm is the matrix or context within which an enquiry proceeds. Specifically in relation to scientific enquiry, it is the assumptions, training methods, standards, goals, methods and expectations that characterize the scientific community at a stable stage of scientific development. Kuhn pointed out that these can change dramatically. For a paradigm, problems that arise may develop into a crisis, leading to a revolution where a new paradigm emerges.

The crucial issue for relativism is the thought that paradigms are incommensurable. It is not possible to adjudicate rationally between competing paradigms because paradigms create the context within which rationality operates. It may well be impossible to even understand paradigms different from one's own. Such a thought leads to a very strong form of relativism, where truth, rationality, what can rightly be said to really exist and so on are all relative to a paradigm. Again, the question of whether Kuhn's own work leads to this conclusion is important (and will be addressed in Chapter 5), but such ideas have currency in many parts of contemporary culture.

This section has presented, so far, some developments in twentieth-century thought that have aided the spread of relativistic ideas, but what cognitive relativism really is hasn't yet been fully clarified. Furthermore, there are important distinctions between kinds of relativism that must be examined. On some issues, nearly everyone is a relativist (consider the old adage "*de gustibus non disputandum est* [there's no accounting for taste]"). However, on others – whether truth is relative, or whether there is a universal standard of rationality – there is much dispute. The final section of this chapter attempts to clarify what relativism is, in general, and distinguish the central kinds of relativism germane to this book.

The cognitive relativism family

Five main kinds of cognitive relativism are distinguished in this book. This is not intended as an exhaustive list of all possible kinds of cognitive relativism, but these five have generated the most interesting discussions. First, there's relativism about truth, which will be rejected. But even if truth is indeed an absolute concept, it will be seen that some other significant issues are still open to the relativizing move. Secondly, relativism about logic will be treated and a limited amount of that allowed. Thirdly, ontological relativism will be presented as an acceptable form of relativism. Fourthly, epistemological relativism will be discussed. This is a more nuanced issue. Some kinds of epistemological relativism are acceptable and some are not. The acceptable kinds are committed to a minimal theory of rationality; the unacceptable ones deny such a minimal theory. The fifth and final kind of relativism is relativism about rationality. A minimal theory of rationality will be defended against relativistic opponents.

This account of the issue is clearly not neutral. An integrated position rejecting some forms of relativism and defending others will be presented. Let us look in some more detail at how the parts fit together. Chapter 2 deals with truth, which many take to be a central issue for discussions of relativism. It will be argued that relativistic notions of truth prove deeply problematical. They tend to either undermine themselves or else covertly collapse into other forms of relativism. However, there is also the issue of our theory of truth. An absolute theory of truth has strong negative implications for other forms of relativism if it is a correspondence theory (hence anti-relativists such as Devitt and Searle strongly push such a theory; see Devitt (1997) and Searle (1995)). Yet with other theories of truth – such as an epistemic or deflationist theory – an absolutist stance doesn't put constraints on logical, ontological or epistemic relativism. Chapter 2 also looks at the issue of alternative logics. In one sense it is obvious that there are many different systems of logic. A system of logic is a formal codification of rules of inference. These rules may be formulated in different ways. Some systems may have axioms as their starting place, and other systems may simply use rules of deduction and no axioms. Some systems may have multiple logical operators, and others may have just one. Yet one might say that all this diversity doesn't add up to genuine relativism, since there is an underlying reality to which all these systems are answerable. This underlying reality is traced to basic logical laws such as the law of non-contradiction, or the law of excluded middle, which set bounds to the diversity possible in the various formal systems. However, logical relativism argues that there may be diversity even at this more fundamental level: some-one may coherently deny these basic laws. This seems really odd, not least because the very idea of coherence is tied up with accept-ing such laws. I shall defend a limited kind of logical relativism. I shall argue that in certain contexts one can be justified in suspend-ing some of the laws of logic. However, such suspensions are limited and the area of discourse so affected is circumscribed by other areas in which the standard laws operate. Thus some logical relativity is allowed, but in a very mitigated sense.

Chapter 3 deals with ontological relativism. Ontology is the part of philosophy that articulates at the most fundamental level what there is. It presents the most basic categorizations of the kinds of things that exist and their properties. An absolutist about this will say that basic facts about ontology are unified and unchanging. The way we think about basic structures in the world is not revis-able in any significant way, once we have achieved a true account. Contenders may abound as to what that account is – but there is only one true account. There may be different reasons offered as to why it is that we have the one true account: it might derive from the nature of the world itself, or it might come from the nature of our mind confronted with a world to which we have no direct access. But the key point is that there is just one true story possible. A rela-tivist rejects this picture. Ontology doesn't present a single unchanging unified view of reality. Facts don't exist totally unaf-fected by the attention, interest and capacities of the observer of those facts. Because observers can have a variety of interests and ways of relating to the world, they can construe facts in different ways, which are not simple variants of each other. Relativists emphasize the constructive role we have in producing ontological theories. Anti-relativists reject this role, often charging the relativist with being some kind of idealist and regarding that as an obviously bad thing. In this chapter, two different approaches to ontological relativity will be examined. One, deriving from Quine, relies on a particular conception of epistemology. Another, from Putnam, has a different model of epistemology. The closing part of that chapter presents criticisms of these and attempts a defence of ontological relativism.

Epistemological relativism is addressed in Chapter 4. It begins by looking in some detail at the question of scepticism and relativism, tracing the development of relativistic thinking in epistemology to certain kinds of response to scepticism. Then, looking at some major debates in contemporary epistemology, we see how relativistic themes are intimately connected to them. Having set the scene in this way, the chapter addresses the position labelled "radical epistemological relativism". Richard Rorty and Steven Stich serve as proponents of this view. They offer different sets of considerations to defend the view that there are no universal criteria by which one can justify any belief. The critical response will be to argue that they have overstated the case. Nevertheless, there is a more moderate form of relativism, which I will defend: relativism about the a priori.

Relativism about the a priori connects directly with conceptual relativity and ontological relativity. Conceptual relativity holds that our concepts are not fixed directly by the nature of the world: we have creative input and can produce better or worse conceptualizations of reality. Better and worse in this context are judged by how successful the concepts are in allowing us to understand and deal with the world. Better concepts – for example, "oxygen" – help us in our theorizing about the world and allow us to predict events in it. Worse concepts – for example, "phlogiston" or "evil spirits" – fail in this respect. It is a pragmatic test.

Our concepts give us our ontology – we talk about the world and pick out features in it that we think are relevant to us. When we determine conditions for the identity of those features we have an ontology. We have different interests that focus on different features of reality, yielding different ontologies. Unlike in the case where one ontology replaces another (as in the winning out of the oxygen story over the phlogiston story in the history of chemistry), we may sometimes hold two sets of ontology in tandem. For example, I may think of myself in terms of a physical organism with a set of definite features. I may also think of myself in other terms, perhaps biographical ones. One isn't reducible to the other. What is central to the position here is that both the world and our interests interact to produce ontologies and systems of concepts. Philosophers who want to argue for an absolutist system of concepts or ontology tend to minimize the role of human interest. Knowledge deriving from the way concepts relate to one another, independent of empirical input, is a priori knowledge. Logic and mathematics are clear examples of this: the meaning of "two", "four", "plus" and "equals" are such that "two plus two equals four" comes out true without any investigation of the world. There are other more complex examples where making the distinction between conceptual knowledge and knowledge of the world gets trickier. For example, is "a physical object exists in space and time" merely conceptual or does it yield a fact about the world? These are issues addressed in Chapter 4.

This debate is a quite traditional epistemological debate. Putting it in the usual language, it is the question about whether there is genuine synthetic a priori knowledge. However, in the way it is approached in Chapter 4, the debate broadens out into a general discussion of rationality. Is there a universal standard of rationality to which all human beings should assent? This is the subject of Chapter 5. Many philosophers have denied that there is one; indeed one could argue that such a denial is characteristic of much later twentieth-century philosophy. They say that there are no universal features that constitute a notion of rationality that is common to all human beings. This viewpoint has been advanced by sociologists of knowledge, by philosophers influenced by Wittgenstein and by many who think Kuhn's work defeated the idea of a general account of rationality. We have many different conceptual schemes, none of which can claim to survey the others in any authoritative fashion. However, others have thought this viewpoint an anathema. Davidson developed a classic rebuttal of such views in his paper "On the Very Idea of a Conceptual Scheme" (1984: 183ff.), arguing that the notion of an alternative conceptual scheme is a contradiction in terms. To recognize something as an alternative conceptual scheme means that it was familiar enough to be recognized as a conceptual scheme, that is as related to our existing conceptual schemes. This argument has generated much debate. In Chapter 5 I argue against the view that there are radical disjunctions between cultures, societies and historical epochs as regards conceptual schemes. There are differences, certainly, and one should beware of assuming that one understands that which superficially seems clear. However, in Chapter 5 I disagree with Davidson's way of doing this: it is too strong. I argue that both rationality and the concepts underpinning our employment of it may mutate and alter. Indeed, it may transmute into something that we, in our culture and epoch, would find very hard to grasp.

The strategy for arguing for lack of disjunction in human rationality is weaker, more modest and accordingly more attractive than Davidson's. Its first point is empirical: the purported alternative conceptual schemes advanced do not, on inspection, turn out to be quite so alternative after all. One doesn't have to defend the view that such an alternative conceptual scheme couldn't be produced – just that no convincing one has been hitherto. This has the advantage over Davidson of being answerable to empirical research, rather than being an armchair edict of impossibility. The second point is that those who argue at a more abstract level for alternative conceptual schemes have tended to do so in a way that is firmly within a familiar mode of reasoning: giving arguments, adducing evidence, clarifying, distinguishing, concluding, and so on. Their cognitive practices contradict the content of what they say. This is not to say that a new approach could never arise, but that one hasn't so far.

A description of a minimal set of principles of rationality, called the core conception of rationality, will be presented. In its minimality the set is compatible with a multiplicity of worldviews and alternative substantive positions. Hence there can be ontological and some logical relativity within the constraints of rational absolutism. This position also accepts that rationality has its limits and there are significant features of our lives beyond those limits. The problem arises when one attempts to characterize whatever is beyond those limits in a rational way, presenting such a characterization as a mode of thinking that constitutes a new or alternative rationality. Whatever is there in this realm – for example the emotional, the aesthetic, the spiritual – can indeed be captured and expressed in language, symbol and gesture. The point is that this is different to what is captured in rational discourse and that it is a mistake to think of this as a new rationality. This is precisely because such a characterization of it tends to be destructive of rational discourse, which is a basic tool universally binding on human cognition.

So the position staked out in this book is one that denies relativism about truth, accepts a great deal of ontological relativity and a lesser amount of logical relativity, resists radical epistemological relativity and denies relativism about reason. Now perhaps an objection to such a position is that it is just a disguised form of scepticism. We never know the real world: our knowledge is just a "put-up job", an invention. Part of the problem with this objection is the weasel word "real", which is often used as a term of approval for a specific area in order to disparage another. Think of business people accusing academics of ignoring the real world, rugged outdoors people disparaging suburbanites, and men wondering whether they should avoid eating quiche, get in touch with their feelings or drink a certain kind of beer to achieve "real" status. What exactly is the real world? One way of describing this is to say that it is a reality independent of our thinking: no thought of ours affects it. Dinosaurs existed prior to humanity and no amount of clever conceptualization on our part alters the reality of dinosaurs, so there is a gap between reality and knowledge – they must be kept separate. However, the irony of this is that such a way of defending objectivity allows the possibility of scepticism. Our knowledge could totally fail to connect with the world as it really is, since there is no necessary connection between knowledge and world. We could simply fail to know anything about the world. On the other hand, if the gap were denied and one held that world and knowledge were intimately connected, then the possibility of such global scepticism would be eradicated. The point is that what at first seems like a sceptical position – that our thinking affects how the world is to us – turns out to be a way of warding off a much more profound form of scepticism (more of this in Chapter 4). My aim here is to characterize relativism as a mid-point between absolutism and scepticism. The absolutist holds that there are facts existing independently of our thought and that no interpretation of ours makes any difference to them. The relativist denies that such a position makes sense and argues that "fact" is a theoretical notion and that facts can be described in diverse ways. The sceptic holds that we can never know facts at all to any degree.

Conclusion

Relativism is an important topic for many disciplines at the start of the twenty-first century. The debates about it are vigorous and tend to be extremely polemical. Defending any form of relativism tends to elicit swift responses along the lines that one is destroying western civilization as we know it. Rejecting relativism provokes responses along the lines that one is socially and politically conservative, if not positively reactionary. Attempting a middle course will no doubt draw flak from both sides of the debate (including, certainly, a rejection of the claim that it is a middle position). Nevertheless, I think it is important to attempt just such a perilous venture. There is much that is good in pro-relativist literature and many criticisms of the more radically relativist stance are also right on target. The limited aims of this book are to:

- distinguish separate claims about relativism in the areas of truth, logic, ontology, epistemology and rationality;
- explore the interconnections between these positions, establishing patterns of coherence among them;
- defend moderate claims for relativism about logic, ontology and epistemology; and
- resist claims for relativism about truth and rationality.

To do this comprehensively a book several times this size would be required but a useful start can be made in what follows.

2 Truth and logic

Much of the negative reaction to relativism is connected to issues about truth and the apparent incoherence of attempting to relativize the notion of truth. The great majority of philosophers have taken for granted the idea that truth and falsity are absolute concepts, whatever else may be relativized. However, there have always been those who rejected this view, holding that truth is indeed relative. Some of these have offered penetrating and ingenious arguments as to how and why the notion of truth should be relativized.

The idea of "truth" is intimately connected to a host of other concepts such as "fact", "reality", "belief" and "knowledge" and is fundamental to most conceptual schemes. Hence any deep alteration to the concept of truth would have a profound knock-on effect in many other areas of philosophy, especially if the alteration construed truth as relative rather than absolute. We can call the kind of relativism associated with truth "alethic relativism" (from the Greek word for truth, *aletheia*). Because truth is so enmeshed with so many other philosophical concepts, the lines of argument concerning alethic relativism get quite tangled. Here, then, are some of the issues that need to be addressed. If truth is relative, then it would follow that something could be true here but not there, or the very same thing that is true today could be not true tomorrow. On the surface this looks like a contradiction, but in fact alethic relativism has often been invoked as a way of avoiding contradiction. First, one needs to get clear about the idea of contradiction. What is it and why is it problematical, if indeed it is? Can one legitimately accept contradictions? This is a starting point for talk about alethic relativism, since a desire to avoid the contradictions that arise from competing viewpoints motivates many relativists about truth. However, since the issue of truth is a semantic one, one also needs to be clear about how exactly alethic relativism differs from epistemological or ontological relativism. What is distinctive about alethic relativism? Investigating contradiction helps sort out these issues.

Furthermore, one must keep clear the distinction between the ascription of truth and the nature of truth. To ascribe truth means to appropriately apply truth or falsity to a belief, sentence or proposition. Questions can arise about what criteria of appropriateness are used, whether they are correct, or whether one has sufficient reason to make the ascription (basically, are you right in calling X true or false?). However, these questions are different from those about the nature of truth. What exactly is truth? Is it a property and if so what kind of property is it? (Basically, what do you mean when you call X true or false?)

In the first section of this chapter, the relation of contradiction to relativism will be discussed, showing how alethic relativism can arise as a way of avoiding contradiction. This will be followed by a discussion of a number of different attempts to present a relativized conception of truth, all of which will be rejected. In the second section the issue of how theories of truth could affect alethic relativism will be treated. It might be possible in some theories of truth to defend alethic relativism (although this would stand as an argument against that theory of truth for many). Finally, in the third section, since issues of logic are deeply connected to questions about truth, the discussion addresses the issue of whether logic is relative. That is, could there be alternative systems of logic?

Alethic relativism

It is a fact that there is a multiplicity of conflicting beliefs in the world. People have widely differing views on, for example, politics, moral issues, religious issues, music, art and so on. One of the motivations of the alethic relativist is to attempt to accommodate this diversity, to countenance the possibility that widely different viewpoints that appear to contradict each other may nevertheless be true. Such a relativist must reject two other possible non-relativist approaches to this diversity. The first, which can be called "dogmatism", selects one of the competitors and holds it true against the rest, declaring them false. The second is limited "non-cognitivism", which holds that truth isn't at issue at all – none of the disputants really have the truth, they are all merely uttering opinions, none of which are genuine candidates for truth. Because truth isn't at issue, diversity can easily exist. This second position presupposes that there are at least some things that are true in a non-relative way (e.g. scientific statements about the world), but others are not candidates for truth or falsity (e.g. value judgements, moral views, religious views, etc). Diversity can flourish when truth isn't in the picture.

The alethic relativist, on the other hand, wants to hold that some or all of these competing views are genuine candidates for truth or falsity and, furthermore, are in fact true, and so rejects both limited non-cognitivism and dogmatism. This is why the issue of apparent contradiction becomes pressing for the alethic relativist. To accept opposing positions as both being true simultaneously is, on the face of it, to accept a contradiction, and to do such a thing seems unacceptable. We need now to see why contradictions *are* unacceptable and then see what is distinctive about alethic relativism as a way of allowing diversity while avoiding contradiction.

A contradiction occurs when someone utters a proposition and its negation at the same time, both being understood in the same respect. The qualifications here are important. People often change their minds and so can utter conflicting views over a period of time, but this is not, strictly speaking, contradiction. They can say, "I believed 'not-*p*' then, but I believe '*p*' now for I was wrong". Furthermore it has to be clear that '*p*' and 'not-*p*' are indeed what is in question: there has to be genuine opposition. For example, I can say, indicating an object, "This is black", and also say "This is white" without contradiction, since there may be black and white objects. However, I cannot say "This is black" and "This is not-black" when referring to the same thing. Now it seems that the relativist cannot avoid doing this if he or she wants to accept the diversity of views mentioned above. But even if it seems that doing this is obviously wrong, what exactly is the problem with holding a contradiction?

The basic problem is that the notion of contradiction is essentially connected to the notions of assertion and negation. When one makes an assertion, one first of all expresses a content and then endorses it as true. This content holds that something in the world is in such a way. Such an assertion also rules out various other things, namely the negation of that assertion. So, for example, if I say the sun is shining, and this is understood in a determinate way (namely relative to a time and place) it rules out a certain opposing state of affairs, namely that the sun is not shining at that time and place. So assertion implies the rejection of the negation of the assertion. But a contradiction makes an assertion and simultaneously asserts the negation of that first assertion. Because of this, a contradiction undermines the very process of making an assertion. To accept a contradiction means to render empty the very act of asserting. Hence contradictions are to be avoided. The basic logical principle forbidding contradiction – the law of non-contradiction – is so basic to reasoning that one cannot argue for it on the basis of anything more fundamental. However, the argument just given tries to show the insurmountable problem for anyone who attempts to deny this law. Any attempt to say anything presupposes this principle. Even denying the principle, in so far as it has any meaning whatsoever, must have a determinate content that is not undermined by simultaneously affirming the principle. So that is why contradictions must be avoided.

How, then, can one hold to the supposed diversity of viewpoints while avoiding contradiction? This is where alethic relativism comes into its own, by denying that contradictions really occur in claiming that truth itself is a relative notion. So when you say "p" and I say "not-p", the former is "true for you" and the latter is "true for me". Truth is relative to the speaker and so true-for-me and false-for-you don't really clash. So you can say "Social democracy is the best form of government", I can say "Social democracy is the worst form of government" and we can both hold to our views, since the former is true-for-you and the latter is true-for-me and no contradiction occurs.

Straightaway there is a burden on the alethic relativist to explain what exactly is meant by this notion of relative truth. How does relative truth relate to absolute truth? Is all truth relative, or is some relative and some absolute? If all truth is relative, is that itself relatively true or absolutely true? As one philosopher has quipped, "You may not be coming from where I'm coming from, but I know relativism isn't *true for me*" (see Putnam 1981: 119). So a great deal of clarification of such a notion is required.

At the crudest level, the notion of relative truth is employed merely as a diffident or polite means of making an assertion. When someone says "God exists is true for me", it simply means that they believe that God exists, but wish to express it in a non-confrontational manner. This then has to be assessed in terms of absolute truth or falsity: they could be mistaken in their belief. As a way of trying to relativize truth, this is a non-starter, although unfortunately it is common enough. Some better way is required and there are a number of different avenues open to the alethic relativist. I shall discuss three here. The first is by the use of artificial languages, which is an approach associated with Tarski and Carnap. The second is by challenging the view that true and false are indeed the only values associated with assertions (the only "truth-values", as it is explained technically), which is a view associated with Joseph Margolis. The third is the account given by Swoyer, which ultimately shifts the relativization away from truth and on to something else, which we will see below.

Artificial languages

The German philosopher Gottlob Frege championed the use of specially constructed languages for philosophy. His contention was that ordinary natural languages are too vague and imprecise for scientific usage. He devised a special kind of language, the *Begriffsschrift* (concept-script) for that purpose. His student and fellow countryman, Rudolf Carnap, followed in his path and devoted a great deal of energy to establishing the syntax and semantics for such languages. In such languages, various philosophical issues that were contentious in ordinary language could be resolved. Notions such as the analytic–synthetic distinction, logical consequence and, most importantly in this context, truth, could be defined clearly in these languages. The properties of these terms could be clearly delineated. Carnap initially advocated a purely syntactical approach to these languages (just using linguistic rules, with no reference to extra-linguistic reality). In so doing, he believed that extraneous problems in epistemology or ontology could be excised from the clear, purely formal account of these notions. Although he subsequently allowed semantic definitions (where extra-linguistic reference comes in), he still maintained that these definitions are neutral with regards to traditional philosophical debates. Such philosophical debates were not genuinely scientific matters and as such were pseudo-debates arising from confusion over language. The task of the new breed of philosopher is to clarify meanings: to build artificial languages that can be tooled precisely to the requirements of the working scientist. Which of these languages will be used by the scientist is a pragmatic issue.

Now the notion of truth, in its normal usage, is one of the sloppy concepts that generates pseudo-debate about, for example, correspondence between appearance and reality. In the new formal languages the concept can be given a strict definition, but this definition is internal to the specific formal language: it only holds within that language. When Tarski developed his celebrated semantic account of truth, he followed Carnap in dealing only with artificial languages. His account doesn't hold for natural language. So the general notion of truth disappears, to be replaced by "true-in-L", where L is the formal language. In this way truth becomes relativized to each artificial language. Contradictions can occur within a language, and the linguistic rules of each language set up what constitutes a contradiction in each one. However, contradictions only occur internally in a specific artificial language; they do not occur across languages. In this manner, truth can be relativized.

The obvious rejoinder to this is to challenge the relevance of such artificial languages and definitions to truth concerning real beliefs. The genuine disputes between people about their beliefs can't be sidestepped by the employment of artificial languages. Such languages might help clarify issues, like building a model, but only if they relevantly connect with the actual ordinary usage. Carnap wanted to maintain that a choice of language was a "pragmatic" issue, which didn't entail any theoretical issues, or raise any questions of truth – it was simply a matter of whether the language was useful or not. However, even to make the judgement that "this language is useful" requires use of the notion of truth – that it's true that the language is useful. Such a notion of truth is not relativized to the artificial language in question, as it stands outside it and is used to pronounce a verdict on it. It is the kind of truth that use of artificial languages tried to remove from theoretical discussion. But such use seems unavoidable. While the building of artificial calculi is indeed possible, they do not help with the genuine substantive problems about truth, conflicting beliefs and relativism. So this avenue for relativizing truth, namely constructing artificial languages, is a dead end.

Multiple truth-values

Conflicting views of the world generate contradictions in the context of the employment of classical logic, which holds to just two truth-values: true and false. Relativistic views of reality are accused of self-refutation in the context of such a view of classical logic. Some philosophers have suggested dropping this requirement as a way of circumventing the problems with relativism. Instead of just two truth-values there may be three or more. This means dropping one of the classical laws of logic, the law of excluded middle, which states that there can be only two truth-values, and no third value is given – *tertium non datur* . What might such a third value be? One standard answer is "indeterminate". Other approaches suggest that there may be multiple values, for example "true", "mostly true", "mainly true", "half true", "mainly false", "mostly false" and "false". Such a schema would have seven truth-values. Even more values are possible using numerical values like a probability calculus, with 1 as true and 0 as false and degrees of truth and falsity given numerical value in between – for example, "0.56 true".

Such a move on its own doesn't immediately constitute relativism. There are advocates of multiple-value logics who don't consider themselves relativists. However, it does give alethic relativists a way of defusing contradictions, since what would be a straight contradiction in two-value logic need not be a contradiction in multiple-value logic. "p" may be very probably or 0.96 true, while "not-p" could be half or 0.5 true and so, it is claimed, a classical contradiction is avoided. Joseph Margolis develops a detailed relativistic position using the rejection of excluded middle as a minimal condition (Margolis 1991). He links this rejection to what he calls "cognitive intransparency": we don't really know a world-in-itself – the world is always mediated to us in historical and context-laden ways. As Margolis explains:

> different investigators (located either synchronically or dia-
> chronically) are, on the available evidence, often unable to
> incorporate an adequate and coherent picture of one another's
> conceptions within the terms of reference of their own.
>
> (1989: 249)

Margolis's contention is that ontological relativity and incommensurability have sometimes been defended using classical logic,
and in such circumstances run into problems of self-contradiction.
Making the move to multiple-value logic avoids this and allows a
robust, non-contradictory relativism.

This position can be challenged in a number of ways. First, one
can query whether there is genuinely a third truth-*value*. It may be
conceded that some propositions are indeterminate, but that is not
to introduce a new truth-value. Rather it is to register a "truth-
gap": an inability to ascribe a truth-value. Logical systems have
indeed been developed with this truth-gap procedure, rather than
advocating a genuinely new truth-value. Secondly, one can query
whether appealing to modifying adverbs like "mostly", "mainly",
"partially" and so on really alters what is meant by true. One can
regard phrases such as "mostly true" as indicating a probability, a
likelihood of truth, but this seems to be an epistemic issue about
how likely something is to be true, rather than importing a new
conception of truth. So the kinds of consideration that lead one to
multiple truth-values can be accommodated within classical logic,
without having to alter it. Thirdly, just as in the case of proponents
of artificial languages advocating "true-in-L", one can query what
exactly is the relationship between the supposed new truth-values
and the standard conception of truth with two truth-values. Is there
anything genuinely explanatory in the new situation and does it
really avoid covertly relying on the traditional conception of truth?

One of the main motivations for ontological relativity, as we
shall see, is, in fact, a desire to avoid contradiction. But this can be
done successfully without our having to alter our conception of
truth. So for reasons of conceptual conservatism (as Quine puts it,
to follow a policy of minimum mutilation) one can keep a classical
conception of truth as absolute, while still having other forms of
relativism and not falling into self-refutation. Hence, for specific
technical reasons about the viability of multiple truth-values and

larger strategic reasons about minimum change to our toolbox of basic concepts, one can keep truth as non-relative, while allowing relativism elsewhere. But there is a third suggested way of relativizing truth.

Strong and weak alethic relativism

Chris Swoyer (1982) investigates the notion of alethic relativism, pointing out that many of the responses to alethic relativism are question-begging, in the sense that they assume an absolute conception of truth in order to refute the relativist, which is precisely what is at issue. A successful refutation of alethic relativism would have to show that absolute truth emerges as a conclusion to the argument, rather than operating as an assumption behind it.

Swoyer initially points out that alethic relativism involves the question of the nature of truth, rather than of criteria for the ascription of truth. He then indicates that discussions of relative truth typically employ the notion of a framework. Relative truth is truth that is relative to some framework. This framework may be of different kinds: historical, cultural, linguistic or biological, for example. The notion of framework need not be given necessary and sufficient conditions – think of it as a "family resemblance" concept. The core issue for alethic relativism is that something that is true in one framework may be false in another framework. The relativization of truth to framework avoids the kind of contradiction that occurs when the same thing is true and false in the same framework. Now this is similar to the suggestion above of true-in-L for artificial languages, except that L is now replaced by the notion of a framework. An example of such a framework is the language of the Hopi Indians.

Swoyer makes an important distinction between two kinds of relativism about truth. Strong alethic relativism holds that the same sentence can be true in one framework, but false in another. For example the Hopi may say "XYZ", which translates as "spirits live in trees". "XYZ" is true in the Hopi framework, but false when translated into normal English. It is important to note that the focus here is on relative notions of truth – not on relative ontologies or relative epistemological standards – so it is truth that is relativized, not criteria for ascribing truth varying with culture, or alternative ontologies. (However, a source of confusion here is that the Hopi do in fact have a different ontology. Swoyer is exploring the possibility of relativism about truth, but it seems better to explain the difference between the Hopi and standard scientific view with a relativized ontology, but keeping an absolute conception of truth.) Relative to the Hopi framework there is truth; relative to standard English there is falsehood. On the other hand weak alethic relativism holds that while a statement may be true in one framework, it is inexpressible in another. There aren't the conceptual resources to state it. So while "PQR" is true in Hopi, no translation is possible into English. This latter kind of relativism raises questions about incommensurability, which will be discussed in Chapter 5. However, Swoyer decides to focus on strong rather than weak relativism, since most of the proponents of framework relativism do actually hold to the possibility of translating from one into another. So a possible candidate for relativism about truth is strong alethic relativism, where a sentence is true relative to one framework, but false relative to another. What is it that allows such relativism to occur?

Swoyer notes that two premises lead to the conclusion that truth is relative. The first is that the world is never accessed as it is in itself. Adherence to some kind of constructivist epistemology holds that the world is partially constituted by the concepts used to mediate it. There is a notion of the world in itself, but it is a limit, or purely formal notion. The second premise is that translation is possible between frameworks, thus blocking off the option of weak relativism. Putting these together, we get:

1. The world as experienced is partially constituted by frameworks.
2. Translation between frameworks is possible.

Hence

3. Truth is relative in the strong sense.

Let us accept for the moment the two premises, 1 and 2 (which will be further discussed respectively in Chapters 3 and 5). Does the conclusion, 3, follow? Swoyer thinks not. The problem is to make sense of how there could be anything in common between the two frameworks that could be true in one and false in another. The problem arises most naturally when you consider two sentences, one that purports to be a translation of the other, where the former is true in F_1 and the latter is false in F_2. In what sense are they the same sentence, or equivalents? If the ontology is different between the frameworks – that is, if the world is different as expressed by the two frameworks – then it seems that the meaning of the sentences must be different. This is so whether you think of meaning as determined by the world (given that the ontologies will be different) or determined by conceptual role (the concepts and their inter-relations differ). As Swoyer pithily puts it, a change of world entails a change of meaning.

This still leaves open the possibility of weak alethic relativism, that truths in one framework may be inexpressible in another. Similar views have been put forward by Ian Hacking (1982). He holds that there may be something prior to the ascription of truth or falsity to sentences, which he calls styles of reasoning. Styles of reasoning are the context in which sentences become candidates for truth or falsehood. Examples of such styles of reasoning are: postulation in mathematical science; experimental method; hypothetical use of analogical models; ordering using taxonomy and comparison; statistical analyses; and historical genetic accounts of phenomena. Such styles of reasoning have specific beginnings and histories, and license certain candidates for truth or falsity. These candidates may not appear in other styles of reasoning. So while a sentence may be true or false in one style of reasoning, it does not occur in another different style. So in a weak sense this may be relativism about truth.

However, this isn't genuine relativism about truth. What is required for relativism is that the same thing be held true and false in different contexts. The difference in context (frameworks, language) is what allows avoidance of strict contradiction. Yet it is not clear that this talk of style of reasoning does generate any genuine likelihood of contradiction occurring. The examples of alternative styles of reasoning seem compatible with each other. Because a statement in mathematics cannot adequately be made in the language of historical explanation does not mean that a potential contradiction is looming. Different things are being discussed, which can be lumped together into a larger account with no contradiction. So relativism about truth isn't defensible in that way either.

Yet it may be possible that some of the various theories of truth proposed by philosophers could yield relativistic results. Having discounted the possibility of relative truth from artificial languages, multiple truth-values, constructive epistemology and styles of reasoning, we can enquire whether some kind of alethic relativism could still be valid in the context of a particular *theory* of truth.

Theories of truth

The twentieth century, more than any earlier period, saw a great proliferation of theories of truth. For example, philosophers defended correspondence, coherence and semantic, epistemic, pragmatic, and deflationist theories of truth, among others. The majority view, for the reasons just covered in the previous section, has been that truth is absolute. Nevertheless, such theories of truth have diverse implications for other forms of relativism. The most important distinction between theories of truth is between those that hold that truth is explanatorily important, playing a crucial role in metaphysics and epistemology, and those that deny the explanatory significance of the concept of truth. The former kind of theory (which I'll call a substantive theory) commits one to the view that truth is some kind of property of beliefs or sentences. The latter kind (a deflationist theory) deflates the role of truth by either making it altogether redundant, or else merely a grammatical device allowing certain kinds of reference (e.g. "everything he said is true"). Since the latter kind makes truth trivial, it has few implications for relativism in other areas. However, if one adheres to the former kind of theory there are indeed implications for relativism in ontology and epistemology. In this section I shall discuss just two kinds of substantive theory of truth – the correspondence and epistemic theories – and then contrast these with the deflationist approach.

The correspondence theory is intuitively plausible and has great antiquity. Indeed, for two millennia it was regarded as the only viable account of truth. Aristotle first encapsulated it by holding that truth is saying "of what is that it is and of what is not that it is not" (*Metaphysics* 1011b26; 1998: 107). This is so obviously right that many regard further discussion as futile. However, obvious and right as it is, it is not a theory, but rather a slogan that needs development. The chief problem for the correspondence theory of truth lies in elaborating the details. The account Wittgenstein presented in his *Tractatus* is often taken as a paradigm instance of a sophisticated correspondence theory of truth. He held there that truth is a correspondence between propositions in language and facts in reality. He explained how propositions relate to reality by means of his picture theory. The elements of propositions (names) stand in one-to-one relation with the basic elements of reality (objects). A proposition shares a common structure with the state of affairs it pictures. When a proposition is true, the picture of reality it presents corresponds to the state of affairs in the world. A false proposition lacks this correspondence: the picture given does not have any state of affairs matching it. More complex propositions are built up using basic propositions and the logical connectives such as "and", "or", "not" and so on. The truth of a complex proposition is dependent on the truth or falsity of its constituent basic propositions and the range of logical possibilities allowable for such a proposition. For example, the truth of "$p \,\&\, q$" is dependent on the individual truth-values of "p" and "q" and is only true when both "p" and "q" are actually true, and false when one or other or both are false.

However, this is an untenable account for many reasons. Language is far less uniform that Wittgenstein envisaged; there is not a layer of basic propositions in natural languages in the manner required by his theory. Furthermore, the key notion of isomorphism is unexplained, or at least explained circularly. In attempting to be clear about the relation between the proposition and fact, one is told that there is a sharing of structure between them. However, what exactly that structure is and how it is shared are both unclear. Another problem is that the theory entails a distinctive ontology of simple unanalysable objects, a position called "logical atomism", which Wittgenstein himself subsequently criticized extensively.

The correspondence theory, if correct, is generally taken to entail that there is a fixed nature to reality captured by our thought and language. Truth involves picking out those things that make up the basic furniture of the world and connecting them appropriately with propositions. Such a picture doesn't allow ontological relativity, committed as it is to there being an ultimate furniture of the world (see Chapter 3). It will also become clear that the strong connection between concepts and reality, required by some versions of the correspondence theory, blocks certain kinds of epistemological relativism (see "Relativism about the a priori", pp. 117–29). So a correspondence theorist will resist most forms of cognitive relativism.

Nevertheless, one may query whether this really has to be the case. It is true that those currently defending correspondence theories of truth, for example Michael Devitt or John Searle, are avowed anti-relativists and explicitly use their correspondence theories to challenge various forms of relativism. Yet could there be a correspondence theorist who held to ontological relativity, that there is no one way the world is, and yet held that truth is correspondence with multiple realities? The attraction of correspondence for its defenders is that it gives a robust, explanatory account of truth and the mind–world relation. This is most compelling when paired with ontological absolutism, giving a powerful explanatory package. The explanatory efficacy of the correspondence theory diminishes greatly if there is the possibility of more than one competing explanatory account of the nature of reality. Evidence for this can be seen by the fact that those who defend ontological relativity (for example, Quine and Putnam) tend to find correspondence unsatisfactory and mystifying, and adopt different accounts of truth, whereas those advocating correspondence tend to be ontological absolutists. So there is no formal argument preventing the linking of correspondence truth with ontological relativism, but it fits more naturally with a robust anti-relativistic realism, where it fulfils an explanatory role.

A different theory of truth, the epistemic theory, is motivated by the desire to avoid negative features of the correspondence theory. The correspondence theory strictly separated truth from knowledge. On the correspondence theory it is possible that all our purported knowledge of the world may turn out to be false, because there is no necessity that our beliefs be true. This allowed the possibility of extreme scepticism: a radical disjunction between thought and reality. Thought could fail to correspond appropriately with reality and so turn out to be false. The world could be wholly other than we think it is. In order to reject this avenue to scepticism, a view of truth was devised that connected it more closely to our thought about the world: the epistemic theory of truth. This presents truth as that which is licensed by our best theory of reality. Truth is cashed out as a function of our thinking about the world; the truth is what is articulated in our best thoughts about reality. An obvious problem with this is the fact of revision; theories are constantly refined and corrected, and so truth would appear to change constantly on that view. To deal with this objection it is suggested that truth be regarded as an ideal: the conclusion reached at the end of enquiry. We never in fact reach it, but it serves as a goal, an asymptotic end of enquiry. Some reject this theory on the basis that it conflates two things that should be kept quite separate. Truth is a metaphysical property of beliefs. How we acquire such beliefs is another question – an epistemological question. To give an account of the metaphysical nature of truth in terms of how we acquire beliefs is to fall into conceptual error: giving an epistemological answer to a metaphysical question. Yet defenders of the epistemic theory respond that this is just an argument by stipulation, a dogmatic assertion. The epistemic theory of truth is not antipathetic to ontological relativity, since it has no commitment to the ultimate furniture of the world and it also is open to the possibility of some kinds of epistemological relativism (see Chapter 4).

Yet could this last point be used as a way back to relativizing truth? If truth is understood as an epistemic property and there is epistemological relativism, couldn't that lead back to alethic relativism? This depends on the extent of epistemological relativism admitted, which in turn depends on the extent of the relativity in rationality one allows. In Chapter 5 there will be an argument for a core conception of rationality, which is universal, and that governs localized conceptions of rationality (which is the kind of epistemological relativism admissible). Extreme versions of epistemological relativism will be rejected in Chapter 4. Localized conceptions of rationality are alternative sets of epistemic rules – much like the example from Hacking of styles of reasoning. These local rationalities are governed by the core conception of rationality and don't genuinely compete with each other. Therefore, if truth is construed on epistemic grounds, it will be the core conception of rationality that will constitute truth, and which will yield an absolute rather than relativist account of truth.

In contrast to substantive theories of truth, deflationist theories attempt to make truth a non-explanatory concept. The Polish logician Alfred Tarski (1902–83), gave an account of truth that, although substantive itself (giving a definition in terms of the semantic notion "satisfaction"), contained an element that was appropriated by those who wanted to deflate the explanatory role of truth. Tarski set up a condition for theories of truth that attempted to capture the intuitive meaning of "true" – that would give a mechanism capturing all those sentences held to be true and rejecting those that weren't. He called this a material adequacy condition and it was expressed in the famous T-sentence schema. The schema can be expressed as $< S$ is true if and only if $p >$. On the left-hand side we have that to be explained (the *explanandum*), and on the right that which does the explaining (*explanans*). Taking any sentence (say "The cat is on the mat") we can distinguish between mentioning that sentence (usually indicated by quotation marks) and actually using it to indicate an actual state of affairs. By putting the mentioned sentence on the left-hand side, and putting that same sentence in use on the right-hand side, we can establish a foolproof way of establishing when it is true. The sentence "The cat is on the mat" is true if and only if the cat is on the mat. The sentence in use gives the conditions that satisfy the requirements for the mentioned sentence being true.

This was not Tarski's own account of truth; he went on to give a more detailed definition, but various others argued that there was no need to do that. There is nothing more interesting or useful to the notion of truth than the T-schema just outlined. All that is relevant in the notion of truth is captured therein. One version of deflationism suggests that "is true" is a redundant phrase, which adds nothing to the mere *assertion* of p. Another version suggests that truth may be useful as a kind of grammatical device. What is common to all these versions of deflationism is that truth has nothing to do with normativity – with giving explanations which might be of use in metaphysics or epistemology. Truth may be an absolute concept, but it doesn't do much work. Hence it plays no role in placing constraints on any other kinds of relativism.

To sum up, in the earlier part of the chapter I argued generally against relative construals of truth and in this section looked at how both substantive and deflationist accounts of the nature of truth impinged on relativized accounts of truth. No compelling reason to relativize truth emerged from examining theories of truth and the reasons given in the first section serve to resist any attempts to do so. However, depending on the differing understandings of the nature of truth, various options open up for other forms of relativism. Correspondence theorists cannot allow much cognitive relativism. Truth plays a significant explanatory role in their theories and places constraints on ontology and epistemology, disallowing relativism. Epistemic theorists hold that truth is substantive, plays some explanatory role in our cognitive economy, but allows relativism about ontology and a certain amount in epistemology. Deflationist accounts of truth make it explanatorily redundant so it has little impact on other forms of cognitive relativism.

Many other issues about the relation between truth and relativism, beyond our scope here, are being explored. For example, there are enquiries as to whether a theory akin to the correspondence theory (one explicitly non-epistemic and non-deflationist) can coexist with ontological relativity (see Lynch 1998). There are investigations of minimalist theories of truth, which are somewhat stronger than deflationist theories, but weaker than most substantive ones. These seem to leave open the possibility that the truth predicate may vary from discourse to discourse (for example the truth predicate used in ethics may differ from that in epistemology (see Wright 2001)). All of these are germane to determining the ultimate status of alethic relativism and how relativism or absolutism about truth impinges on other forms of relativism.

Relativism about logic

Intimately connected to the discussion of truth is the question of logic, because of the centrality to it of the notions of coherence and contradiction. (This way of thinking about logic has been challenged by some philosophers who hold that inference rather than truth is the most salient feature for understanding logic. I shall not deal with this approach mainly because of limitations of space, but also because the majority position links truth and logic.) Indeed, I needed to mention some logical laws, namely non-contradiction and excluded middle, in discussing alethic relativism in the previous section. If truth is construed as absolute, could there nevertheless be alternative systems of logic? Or is there a single basic system of logic that is the correct one for everyone?

Logic is clearly fundamental to human reasoning. It governs the process of inferring between beliefs in a truth-preserving way, such that if one starts with true beliefs and then makes no mistakes in logic, one is guaranteed to have true beliefs as a conclusion. The central notion of logic, validity, is usually characterized in this fashion. A valid argument is one such that, if the premises are true, the conclusion has to be true. Aristotle was the first to codify logical laws and principles, despite the fact that they had been used in practice well before him. This codification is the mark of logic as a formal discipline. Formal logic systematizes, articulates and regiments the inferences we use in our everyday reasoning processes, distinguishing valid argumentative forms from fallacious reasoning. Aristotle's account of these forms was so successful that, two thousand years later, Kant believed that logic was a completed science. However, the nineteenth century saw this change. Developments in mathematics led to renewed attempts to codify logic. The most significant of these was Frege's formal development of the *Begriffsschrift* (concept-writing), which inaugurated modern symbolic logic. This new system of logic was more sophisticated than Aristotle's in that it could deal with the theory of relations and generality in such a manner that it could be argued that mathematical truths derive from logic truths. Whitehead and Russell further developed this approach (called logicism) in their monumental *Principia Mathematica* (1910–1913), first articulating a logical system and then showing the derivation of mathematical truths from it.

In the aftermath of *Principia*, various alterations and modifications of its basic system were suggested. For example, while Russell and Whitehead had used five primitive logical symbols in their system, Ludwig Wittgenstein suggested reducing these to one, in his *Tractatus Logico-Philosophicus*. He showed how the theorems generated in the system of *Principia* using five logical constants could be generated by repeated use of his single logical constant. However, while Wittgenstein's emendation preserved the spirit of the *Principia* enterprise, it became clear that very different systems could also be generated. On a purely formal level there was no limit to the number of alternative systems that could be generated; one just set up a new set of symbols and a new system of rules of inference and a new system appeared. This kind of system was called a "syntactic system", since there was no reference to anything outside the system: it was a purely formal system. However, when one started relating such systems to things beyond themselves – when the symbols of such a system were interpreted (or given a semantics, i.e. a meaning) – then constraints appeared for such systems. How did such systems relate to the pre-systematic or ordinary person's practices of inference and argument, which logical codifications are supposed to express?

As logicians and mathematicians began to develop a plethora of such systems and offered various semantic interpretations of them, it became clear that some of these were at considerable variance with the classical system expressed in *Principia* and, apparently, with regular pre-systematic usage. *Principia* held to the two fundamental laws of logic as presented by Aristotle: the law of non-contradiction and the law of excluded middle. The law of non-contradiction holds that a proposition and its negation cannot both be true together. So it denies that in a logical system there could be a theorem of the form "p & not-p", or, equivalently, it asserts "not (p & not-p)". The law of excluded middle holds that all propositions are either true or false: there is no third truth-value. As we have seen, both these issues arose in the first section of this chapter, on truth, and I argued there for retention of both these laws. Nevertheless, logicians experimented with systems where these were abandoned. By jettisoning excluded middle, one could develop three-valued or multiple-valued logic. It is quite obvious that a consistent calculus of such a kind is possible. The core question about such calculi is whether they count as logic or not. Can they serve as adequate expressions of pre-systematized inferential practice? Before tackling this question, the extent of the difference between such systems and classical logic needs clarification. What marks out the difference between a minor emendation of classical logic and a full blown alternative logic?

Susan Haack (1996) has usefully distinguished between logical systems that can be understood as rivals to classical logic and those that merely supplement it. A logical system consists minimally of a set of symbols whose use is established by means of syntactical rules plus rules for relating these symbols with one another (i.e. transformation rules), these symbols being called well-formed formulas or wff's. This is a syntactical characterization, which has no bearing on what the expressions stand for, or on truth preservation. The semantical characterization says that the truth of the initial axioms is preserved by rules of consequence that yield logical truths. Now, two systems of logic are merely notational variants of one another when they share the same set of syntactic and transformation rules and theorems, but have different symbols. There is no question at all of rival systems here: the difference is similar to that between using Arabic or Roman numerals in mathematics.

An initial level of difference arises when two systems (let's call them A and B) share some but not other elements. System A has a certain set of symbols and rules that is shared by B. However, B has further symbols and further theorems that are not shared with A. If the logical system in B has greater powers of expression than that in A, B can be called an "extended logic". An extended logic doesn't clash with the earlier classical system – it just adds to it. An example of this could be if B is a modal logic, with expressions for necessity and possibility.

A further difference is manifest where A and B share wff's but differ in theorems produced, and therefore have different rules of inference. If A is classical logic, B will be a "deviant logic": it differs radically from A. Examples here include three-valued logics and quantum logic, where certain classical rules are discarded in favour of different ones. Now, some deviant systems are proposed as wholesale replacements for classical logic. For example, a supporter of three-value logic may claim that it is a superior system to classical two-value logic and hence should replace it in all contexts. This doesn't lead to logical relativism, as there is just one correct formalization of logic – the new three-valued one. It is a question of determining which one is the one true system of logic. Logical relativism emerges if one defends the existence of two or more rival systems that one may legitimately choose between, or move back and forth between. What reasons could there be for making such a move?

Haack has distinguished four different sorts of consideration that might lead one to adopt a rival logic. The first is a "general metaphysical reason". An example of this can be found in intuitionistic logic, which was devised by Brouwer (see Mancosu 1998). He disagreed fundamentally with Russell on the nature of logic and mathematics, holding that mathematics was a fundamental kind of thinking performed by humans, which existed in a pre-linguistic fashion in the mind and for which linguistic representation was inessential. He rejected Russell's view that mathematics derived from logic. Because of this conception of the nature of mathematical knowledge, Brouwer held that it made no sense to postulate mathematical realities that could exist independently of a judging mind. The very nature of mathematics was that it was constructed by an intellect. Therefore, purported mathematical truths that were unknowable by any mind didn't exist; in the realm of mathematics, to be is to be judged to be. Now, an unrestricted application of the law of excluded middle has the result that there are some truths that are either true or false while simultaneously being actually unjudged by the mind. We are not aware of them, but it is a fact that they are either true or false. This cuts against Brouwer's mind-dependent conception of mathematics so he rejects the law of excluded middle. The intuitionistic system of logic does not have this particular law, and therefore constitutes an alternative logical system.

The second is a "desire to avoid philosophical problems". Brouwer's espousal of an alternative logical system derived from a positive antecedent philosophical commitment. One may also be inclined to such systems out of a desire to avoid philosophical commitments that are regarded as troublesome or problematical. The classic example of such a commitment is fatalism: the doctrine that events are predetermined and unamenable to free will. One version of fatalism seems to arise from accepting the law of excluded middle. It is either true or false that I will be knocked down by a car tomorrow. Even though I have no way of knowing which, it is the case that one of these options is a determinate fact. Now, the fatalist argument goes that since what happens tomorrow is a determinate fact (because only one of the options is true) then nothing I can do will alter that fact. This peculiar result seems due to acceptance of the law of excluded middle. Various ways are available by which one might try to avoid this consequence. For example one can deny that truth or falsity applies to things that have not yet happened and so avoid the conclusion of fatalism. But this has its own price: I can't say that "the sun will rise tomorrow" is true, or "global warming will increase by 10 per cent next year". So denial of the law of excluded middle seems to be one way of defusing the fatalist's position that still allows that some future statements are true or false.

The third is a "desire to avoid scientific problems". The previous two cases dealt with the law of excluded middle. The next gets closer to the law of non-contradiction, which some (e.g. the intuitionists) have thought a more fundamental law than the law of excluded middle. Nevertheless, in certain contexts philosophers have been led to drop classical inference rules, because the implications of them in tandem with well-confirmed scientific theories have been unacceptable. This occurs primarily in the context of quantum theory. Particles at the quantum level behave in ways not describable in the standard laws of logic. In the phenomenon known as "superposition", particles are emitted from a source and have two possible routes to take. However as David Z. Albert relates, something most peculiar occurs:

> So what we're faced with it this: Electrons passing through this apparatus, in so far as we are able to fathom the matter, do not take route h and do not take route s and do not take both of these routes and do not take neither of these routes; and the trouble is that those four possibilities are simply all the logical possibilities that we have any notion whatsoever of how to entertain! (1994: 11)

In the face of such phenomena, one can either attribute very strange, almost magical properties to the foundations of matter – or else change the logic in which it is discussed. Such a logic – quantum logic – drops what are called the classical distribution laws, namely that from "p and (q or r)" we can infer "(p and q) or (q and r)". Changing this rule dramatically simplifies the explanation in the physics.

The fourth is a "desire for logical innovation". It is quite possible to develop a formal logical system that accepts contradictions and hence that drops the law of non-contradiction. One can develop the syntactic rules that allow this, and one can develop semantics that cope with this. The usual reaction to such systems is that they are a curiosity, of no actual use. However, some paraconsistent logicians (supporting strongly deviant logics) have argued that such systems are valuable and that they may be of use in getting to understand the nature of paradox, distinguishing between systems that let all consequences follow from a contradiction and those that do not, their interest being in the latter (see Priest 1985/86).

So we have a clearer conception of what is at stake. There are in existence various calculi that deviate from the calculus of classical logic. Do these count as alternative logics, or are they mere formal curiosities? We have seen good reasons motivating some philosophers to adopt such logics, so they are not merely trivial mathematical or logical games. Perhaps the best way of determining this question is to examine some of the objections that have been deployed against such alternative logics.

Various authors hold that classical two-valued logic has a pre-eminence. For example, the influential historians of logic, W. Kneale and M. Kneale, hold that:

> even from the purely formal point of view the ordinary two-valued system has a unique status among deductive systems which can plausibly be called logic, since it contains all the others as fragments of itself. In short, they are not alternatives to classical logic . . .   (1962: 575)

But this can and has been challenged. There are systems that do not readily fit into two-valued logic – where truths expressed in the multi-valued system either do not appear or, indeed, cannot appear in the classical system. Also, the supposedly distinctive position of two-valued logic seems to be merely historical. It is what most people have been used to, but traditional usage is not a good argument for blocking philosophical innovation.

However, W. V. Quine has developed an influential argument against deviant logic, known as the "translation argument". His former student Donald Davidson has further pushed this argument into a general case against alternative conceptual schemes. I shall discuss Davidson's position in "Davidson's argument", pp. 163–70) and I shall also discuss Quine's general epistemological position in more detail in Chapter 3 ("Arguments for ontological relativism", pp. 63–9). However, here I shall present the translation argument and comment on some troublesome features of it.

The background to Quine's argument is the logical positivists' views on logical truth. They had attacked accounts resting on some notion of "intuition". Such accounts posited a special form of knowledge, distinct from empirical knowledge, that allowed one to grasp a priori truths. Many different schools accepted such a doctrine: Neo-Kantians articulated a version of this position, as did Russell. The positivists rejected such a doctrine as mystificatory: it explained the obscure by the more obscure. Instead they began to appeal to the structures of language as a means of making sense of logic. A main source of inspiration in this enterprise was Wittgenstein's account of language in the *Tractatus*, where he presented logical truths as tautologies, which are vacuously true in that they are true no matter what content is supplied for their variables. The positivists advanced a linguistic theory of logical truth, holding that logic derives from linguistic rules. The actual details of this theory are complex since various versions of it, offering different kinds of epistemological grounding for logic, were advanced. Quine's main philosophical mentor, Rudolf Carnap, advanced a version of this doctrine and Quine came to reject it. He accepted the critique of intuition-based accounts of logic, but came to think that in relation to the linguistic theory of logical truth, "there was less to it than meets the eye" (Quine 1970: 95). Logic is so basic to our thinking that nothing more fundamental could explain it. The purported explanation, or "theory" of logic, merely comes to the point that it is obvious. Anyone who correctly understands the language in question will just assent to a logical truth as an obvious truth. A by-product of this view is that it makes no principled distinction between logical truths and other highly general obvious truths. So with this view of logic, what about alternative systems of logic?

Quine accepts the diversity seen in textbooks of logic. These, he holds, are different ways of producing the same set of logical truths, whether by axiomatic method, or proof procedure. Such diversity is relatively trivial. A more substantial form of diversity is to claim different such sets of logical truths (to claim a deviant logic, as discussed above). Quine's initial (and subsequent) response is to say that such a position is absurd, given the basic role of logic in our thinking. Suppose someone asserts "*p* and not-*p*". We would think that such a person had given a different meaning to the terms "and" and "not", rather than genuinely offering a deviant logic. As Quine says, "Here, evidently, is the deviant logician's predicament: when he tries to deny the doctrine he merely changes the subject" (1970: 81). This is the core of the translation argument. We never have good reason to impute deviancy rather than mistranslation. Compare Hume's argument against miracles: we are never in a rational position to accept a miracle, since the evidence will always be stronger in favour of some other explanation than a supernatural one. Likewise, the evidence for wilful distortion or confusion and error is always going to be greater than the imputation of deviancy.

This is a very strong case against deviant logic. However, just as with Hume against miracles, it is quite conservative in its implications. In the case of Quine, the argument seems to exclude in an a priori manner the possibility of deviant logic. The irony in this is that Quine is renowned for his rejection of the a priori. Indeed, in earlier work (Quine 1953) he defended the view that no belief is in principle unrevisable. However if everything is revisable, it is not acceptable to separate logic for special consideration, especially in the context of denying that logic has a different epistemological status to empirical science. We will examine the details of that position in some more detail below in "Arguments for ontological relativism" (pp. 63–9). What is apparent is that there is a tension in Quine's work between the liberal position of 1953 and the conservative position of 1970. The precise interpretation of Quine's position is a delicate and disputed issue. However, I merely wish to signal here the problematical nature of the translation argument, even in the context of Quine's own work.

There are problems for Quine's translation argument on other grounds as well. The argument assumes the initial, antecedent obviousness of classical logic. However, an intuitionist logician might contend that their system is the obviously correct one and that whatever evidence there is for translating the logical utterances of persons points in the direction of a denial of the law of excluded middle. Quine's argument merely states that one translates linguistic behaviour using a base logic, but it doesn't give an independent argument as to whether this is classical or deviant logic. Furthermore, one might question whether looking at considerations about translation, as Quine does, is the most appropriate way of deciding the issue. Quine uses this method because of his own epistemological commitments to empiricism and behaviourism. He doesn't believe that there are any resources available to philosophers to evaluate such questions other than what is observable: linguistic utterances and associated behaviour. One might challenge this and say that empirical evidence from behaviour is not an appropriate way to determine the nature of logic. In rejecting such behaviourism, an opponent might hold that there may be a metaphysical underpinning to logic that is more secure than the empiricist approach (see e.g. Bonjour 1998).

So the arguments against deviant logic are not unambiguously successful. However, there is one further point that appears to be significant. Even if one accepts a deviant system and believes there are good philosophical grounds for defending it, there seem to be general regulative principles governing the choice of a logical system. These include consistency, coherence, simplicity, efficacy and so on. Our choice of logical system is itself governed by a more general conception of rationality. Which notions of logic operate in such a system? In Chapter 5 I shall argue that the law of non-contradiction holds there. Even though I won't argue for this, it would seem plausible that for reasons of simplicity one might hold to a two-valued logic, which doesn't require any alteration in the concept of truth.

Where does that leave the legitimacy of deviant logic? It is clear that multiple-valued systems are possible. It also seems that they have legitimacy in so far as there is a philosophical rationale for their use and no compelling formal argument against them. However, the meta-level that governs the adoption of such systems is committed to at least the law of non-contradiction and probably, for reasons of simplicity, to the law of excluded middle (lower-level contexts requiring suspension of this). To require the existence of such a meta-level is to argue for the existence of a core conception of rationality, which will be argued for in Chapter 5. This is an absolute conception, governing degrees of diversity beneath it. So the upshot of this discussion is that there are legitimate alternative logical calculi, useful for various purposes, but ultimately governed by a system adhering to the traditional laws of logic.

3 Ontological relativism

What is ontological relativism?

Ontology is that part of philosophy which investigates the fundamental structures of the world and the fundamental kinds of things that exist. Terms like "object", "fact", "property", "relation" and "category" are technical terms used to make sense of these most basic features of reality. Until Kant, there was widespread agreement on the framework for debates about ontology, and varying accounts of existence, essence, substance and property were articulated and defended. This involved some of the great debates of Western philosophy, for example about the status of universals. However, amid these differences were shared aims (finding out the fundamental nature of reality) and shared methods (dialectical argumentation). Those philosophers who abstained from these debates did so from the position of scepticism, holding that we just don't have the cognitive wherewithal to decide any of these issues. Nevertheless, there was clear agreement on all sides that ontology had to do with portraying the nature of reality: telling it as it really is. Kant upset this consensus. His Copernican revolution introduced a new dimension to the debate. His suggestion was that ontology has to do with articulating the nature of reality *as known to human cognition*, not *as it is in itself*. In common with sceptics he denies our access to a world in itself. However, unlike sceptics, he believes there is still a point to doing ontology and still an account to be given of the basic structures by which the world is revealed to us. In recasting the very idea of knowledge, changing the object of knowledge from things considered independently of cognition to things in some sense constituted by cognition, Kant believed he had given a decisive answer to traditional scepticism. Scepticism doesn't arise under the new conception of knowledge, since scepticism trades on the possibility of being mistaken about objects in themselves. However, those resisting the Kantian revolution argue that it is precisely sceptical in the fact that it relinquishes our grasp on things independent of mind. This dichotomy led to the great modern debate that is generally called the realist–anti-realist debate. On one side are those explaining objectivity in terms divorced from considerations of mind, pressing the case of a world prior to cognition, which has its own structure and properties independent of mind. On the other are those who emphasize the creative power of mind, putting the case forward that the world is constituted, in varying degrees, by mind. The debate is many faceted and covers many areas. For instance, one might hold that physical objects are real but colours are mind-dependent – being realist about the former and anti-realist about the latter. Or one might hold that numbers are real entities but on the other hand minds are fictional constructs. Again, one might think that electrons really exist but physical laws are constructs, and so on. The list is lengthy. The central issue in the debate is to explain precisely what "real" means and the complexity of the debate is a result of the diversity of answers. How does this realist–anti-realist debate bear on the question of relativism?

The issue is whether "real" is an absolute notion or a relative one. Wolterstorff gives the example of "being a descendant of" to illustrate the difference (1987: 240). This property cannot exist in isolation but is a relational one; it makes no sense to attribute it in a non-relative fashion. Similarly the question is whether "existence", "reality", "the world" and so on are absolute concepts, or are they relative to something else, perhaps a conceptual scheme? Are reality and existence such that there is a single absolute way they are, or are they such that they vary relative to some factors, such as how we conceptualize them? Is reality ordered with a fundamental furniture of the world, or are there a variety of different, but equal ways the world is, that are irreducible to each other? Are these alternatives in the world independent of human cognition, or are they somehow dependent on cognition? These ontological questions are clearly very closely linked to the issue about the relation of our thought to reality. Given the obvious truth that we think of the world in a multiplicity of different ways, how does this bear on the question of an absolute or relative account of reality? If one holds that mind constitutes the world, then perhaps the diversity in thought does indeed have an impact on reality itself. Denying that mind has any impact on the deep nature of reality makes it easier to defend an absolute conception of reality. These are issues that go to the heart of contemporary philosophy. In the next few pages I shall attempt to clarify some of them a little further in order to shed light on ontological relativity – the view that reality has multiple, non-equivalent and irreducible ways of being.

The pre-Kantian position discussed above – that the world had a definite, fixed, absolute nature that was not constituted by thought – has traditionally been called "realism". When challenged by new anti-realist philosophy it became an important issue to try to fix exactly what was meant by all these terms: realism, anti-realism, idealism and so on. Before Kant there had been positions that were called "idealist" – for example, different kinds of neo-Platonism or Berkeley's philosophy. In these systems there is a downplaying or denial of material reality in favour of mind. However, the kind of mind in question, usually the divine mind, guaranteed the absolute objectivity of reality. There is indeed an ultimate furniture of the universe – it just doesn't involve matter. So, in contrast with post-Kantian anti-realism, neo-Platonism and Berkelian idealism accepted an ultimate furniture of the world. Kant's idealism differs from these earlier idealisms in blocking the possibility of discussing this ultimate furniture. The mind discussed by Kant is the human mind (in contrast to the divine mind used by earlier idealists) and it isn't capable of grasping the fundamental features of reality. Indeed, such topics are unthinkable by us, or by any rational being. So Kant's version of idealism results in a form of metaphysical agnosticism. Realism, on the other hand, is faith in our ability to think about and form true beliefs about these fundamental features. Wittgenstein followed Kant's position in his *Tractatus*, where he articulated a linguistic version of this kind of agnosticism. When we attempt to go beyond the limits of what is sayable, we speak nonsense. What sets the limits on what is sayable? For Wittgenstein it was set by the picture theory of language; when picturing (in his sense) occurs, then we can have sensible discourse. The logical positivists developed this further, tying in an empiricist account of picturing through the principle of verification. This gave a means of judging whether what is being uttered is meaningful or meaningless. From such an account of meaning, any attempts to talk about the ultimate furniture of the world were judged meaningless. So post-Kantian metaphysical agnosticism found a variety of quite different forms, all defending the inexpressibility of traditional metaphysical beliefs, but relying on different arguments to do so.

However, this denial of our ability to discuss the ultimate nature of reality is still ambiguous, because it could be understood in two ways. On the first interpretation there is a way the world is in itself, but we humans can't make any sense of it (with the possibility perhaps that beings with higher forms of intelligence can understand it). On the second interpretation it is just meaningless for anyone to think of the ultimate way the world is – such an idea is an empty formula, not signifying anything. The first interpretation shares with realism the ontological claim that there is a way the world is, independent of human cognition. It disagrees with realism on the epistemological claim of our ability to access it. The second interpretation disagrees with realism on ontology – that the notion of the ultimate furniture of the world makes any sense, thus rendering redundant the second question of whether we can know it. Contemporary ontological relativists take the second interpretation. The second interpretation also has the result of changing our understanding of the relationship between ontology and epistemology; it makes no sense to discuss ontological issues as if they were independent of our means of grasping them.

Just as Kant had believed that there was still important work to be done, even after denying the meaningfulness of traditional "furniture of the world" ontology, so too do contemporary anti-realist philosophers. Kant wanted to investigate the conceptual structures by which we access reality, by which a world becomes manifest to us. For Kant, this set of structures is fixed and universal. All humans (and, on certain interpretations, all rational beings) must fit in with these structures. Contemporary anti-realists also want to investigate the conceptual structures by which we understand the world. However, unlike Kant, many of them hold that there is no single universal set of such structures that is necessary for cognition. They defend the view that there are different such structures, and in so doing there are different realities constituted by their use.

This means that reality varies with the concepts deployed – and in this sense it is relative. However, it is most important to remember that the term "reality" is being used here in its post-Kantian agnostic sense. These philosophers believe that the notion of the ultimate way things are is a mistaken notion. So they will not accept the objection that they are really covert idealists – where mind creates reality – because such a view is one of the traditional, pre-Kantian views they have rejected. Rather they argue that they have recast the discussion of the relation of mind to reality by dropping the picture that mind and reality are two separate entities requiring linkage. Mind and reality both emerge as issues to be discussed in the new agnostic landscape. There is no question of attempting to relate these to an antecedent "way things are", or furniture of the world.

Yet there is a significantly different way of thinking about these issues that challenges anti-realism, but still accepts a certain kind of relativism. This proposes a relativism in our theories about the world, but holds firmly to the belief that the world exists independently of our thought about it. That is, there is a way things are, but there are multiple ways of theorizing about it, or describing it. Many defenders of realism hold that this is quite a sensible form of relativism and that it is totally compatible with realism. I can talk about some reality (e.g. a human being) and describe it in terms of physics, biology, history, sociology and so on. These descriptions don't have to be reducible to each other or to some fundamental description. Nevertheless, there is an objective fact of the matter about that reality that is independent of any theory about it. Various other kinds of realist had argued for reductionism about our theories of the world – that there is a fundamental kind of theory that has a privileged place in discussing the world. For example, a modern version of this kind of realism holds that physics articulates the ultimate furniture of the universe and that all other theories are less real than that and need to be appropriately connected to physics to be intellectually respectable. The fundamental nature of the world is uniquely captured by a physical theory, whereas history, economics and biology, say, are derivative and less close to the deep nature of reality than physics. Resisting that form of absolutism about theory led people to reject realism itself. In wanting to deny the sort of intellectual hegemony given to physics, anti-realist philosophers denied the view that there is a fundamental nature to reality. However,a sophisticated realist can argue that this is a mistake. One can accommodate relativity about theory, a non-hierarchical view of our descriptions of the world, yet still hold to the objective existence of the world discussed. It is not constructed by our theories, but rather our theories mediate it to us. Now ontological relativists reject this. Their relativism is of a deeper order. It is not merely that we have different theories about the same facts, but that the facts themselves are actually constituted by different theories. So ontological relativists are anti-realists in the strong sense I have described above; they hold as meaningless the view that our theories carve nature at the joints, so to speak. Both the ontological relativist and the sophisticated realist accept a relativity in theory about the world. They accept that there are multiple irreducible accounts of reality. In this they differ from what we can call naïve realists, who argue for a tight fit between a particular kind of theory and reality (such as the philosopher advocating physics above). The sophisticated realist differs from the ontological relativist in holding that the different theories are about the same thing, whereas the ontological relativists deny the meaningfulness of this idea.

But how can such ontological relativism to be explained? It seems a bizarre doctrine, where reality changes as we think differently about it, resulting, despite protestations, in a very crude form of idealism. In the next section I'll look at specific arguments from Quine and Putnam and look at their particular forms of ontological relativism. For the moment I shall try to give some general characterization of ontological relativist positions. The basic claim common to all these positions is that it makes no sense to speak of a world as it is in itself. Earlier forms of relativism relied on an epistemological argument for this. Verificationists such as Carnap denied the meaningfulness of traditional ontology and only accepted factual statements that could be connected in some form or other to sense experience (Carnap 1959). However, this verificationist view came under severe attack. On the one hand, it was attacked by empiricists, friendly to the thought of banishing traditional metaphysics, but unfriendly to the analytic–synthetic distinction, which Carnap's notion of a factual statement depended on. On the other, it was challenged as a piece of empiricist dogmatism by those unimpressed by empiricist epistemology and rejected as both internally incoherent and externally unfounded. Post-positivistic philosophers who rejected traditional realist metaphysics needed to find some kind of argument, other than verificationism, to reject it. They found such arguments in philosophy of language, particularly in accounts of reference. Explaining how language relates to reality offers a way of attacking the idea that there is a reality structured independently of thought. The main idea is that the structures and identity conditions we attribute to reality derive from the language we use and that such structures and identity conditions are not determined by reality itself, but from decisions we make. Because of this, it is never possible to claim that some particular set of structures and identity conditions are revelatory of reality in itself; they are rather revelatory of the world-as-related-to-by us. The identity of the world is therefore relative, not absolute.

These relative identities need to be further explored. As I have indicated, we have two main competing positions. The first holds that our theories about reality are relative, but reality itself is objective and has an essential identity. The second holds that relativity goes all the way to reality, in fact denying the theory–reality dichotomy. At first the former seems a better position to hold. It retains the relativity of theory that non-reductionists want, but also holds to the objectivity of reality. It doesn't get enmeshed in the strange view that reality itself changes as theory changes. However, the anti-realist can respond to this by first asking what one can say about the reality underlying theory. If all theories are relative and no one is superior to another, then how do we have cognitive access to this underlying reality? To suggest that we can postulate it means that we must have some privileged theory from which we can do so, but we have denied such a privileged theory. So it seems that the sophisticated realist must either retreat back to naïve realism and advocate a basic theory that gets at reality in its essential identity, or retain the relativity of theory but do so by going anti-realist. In the anti-realist model we have theories about the world that are incompatible with each other and that are irreducible to each other. That is, they can't be concatenated together into a grand theory that articulates the ultimate way things are. An example, often cited, is that of wave–particle duality. Such a description postulates incompatible properties to reality. However, we don't say one is basic and reduce the other to it, but rather alternate between them, in a flip-flop fashion. To reject one would mean diminishing our capacity to understand the world. Another example is the split between a scientific austere, deterministic, law-governed account of the universe and an account that incorporates biography, free-will, creativity and spontaneity. Although they are strictly incompatible, we can take different stances on the universe using these different families of concepts. Why? Because we find them indispensable. Our understanding would be greatly impoverished by dropping either group or attempting to reduce one to the other.

However, a problem that rapidly surfaces for relativistic anti-realist arguments is that there are obviously curbs and limits on what we can decide and the most appropriate explanation of these curbs appears to be the nature of the world itself. Reality has a nasty tendency to thwart our decisions, so how exactly are we supposed to be able to decide on structures and identity conditions in reality? For example, if I am fixing my car and am attempting to reach a particularly inaccessible part of the engine, surely it is the structure of the engine itself that makes it so difficult to reach, and not some decision on my part. The realist argues that anything other than this view is a crazy form of hubris – a kind of Promethean anti-realism where we make up the world as we go along. To develop this critical point I would like to discuss the views of Michael Devitt, who has trenchantly defended realism and attacked various forms of anti-realism as unfounded, particularly relativistic anti-realism.

Devitt presents his views in *Realism and Truth* (1997), splitting the work into an initial exposition of his own views and following that with critical polemics against various forms of anti-realism and relativism. At the very beginning of the work he sets out various axioms that are fundamental to his position. They emphasize certain distinctions that he holds to be fundamental to a correct understanding of the issues. The first is to distinguish constitutive and evidential issues in connection with realism. That is, one must clearly separate questions about what exists from questions about how we come to know what exists. In similar fashion one must separate metaphysical from semantic issues. That is, questions about ontology are independent of questions about truth and reference. So Devitt holds that ontology must be treated independently of any issues in semantics or epistemology and that the basic question about realism must be settled before these questions. This basic question is whether things exist independently of mind or not, and the answer to this doesn't involve any issues in epistemology or semantics. This is the core of Devitt's position, the stance from which he takes on anti-realists and relativists and is summarized in the following three maxims:

1. In considering realism distinguish the constitutive and eviden-tial issues.
2. Distinguish the metaphysical (ontological) issue of realism from any semantic issue.
3. Settle the realism issue before any epistemic or semantic issue.

Two subsequent maxims hold that one mustn't take the question of truth for granted in semantics (Devitt wants to defend a substantive explanatory notion of truth as correspondence) and that truth as correspondence is distinct from any epistemological issue. The central thread running through all this is to distinguish clearly ontological issues from semantical and epistemological issues. Ontology doesn't rest on either of the other two, and semantics doesn't rest on epistemology. Therefore he holds that Kantian epistemological attacks on traditional ontology are mistaken and subsequent semantical lines of assault are likewise wrong. But given that anti-realists will just deny these maxims, what is Devitt's case for them?

His fundamental strategy is to argue that they must be accepted as a default position. The position they amount to he calls "common-sense realism", expressed as

> From an early age we come to believe that such objects as stones, trees and cats exist. Further, we believe that these objects exist even when we are not perceiving them and that they do not depend for their existence on our opinions or on anything mental. (Devitt 1997: 60)

No issues about how we come to know these things, or the way language refers to them, should impinge on our assertion of these existing things. He holds that such a view is compelling and almost universally held outside philosophical circles. This doesn't mean it should be accepted uncritically, but one should only reject it in the face of compelling arguments against it and for a plausible alternative. Devitt's contention is that there are no such arguments and no such alternative exists. Therefore his collection of maxims does operate as a default position. Because of this strategy much of his energy goes into analysing and dispatching attempts to get rid of realism. Nevertheless, he does present some positive independent arguments for the realist position. Common-sense realism holds that most of the entities we think exist in a common-sense fashion really do exist. Scientific realism holds that most of the entities postulated by science likewise exist, and the existence in question is independent of any constitutive role we might have. The hypothesis of realism explains why our experience is the way it is. We experience the world thus-and-so because the world really is that way. It is the simplest and most efficient way of accounting for our experience of reality. He describes it as an overarching empirical hypothesis: it might be wrong. That is, it may turn out that what we think exists really doesn't exist, but something else does. While we now think that electrons exist, in the future we might regard this as a mistaken view, akin to belief in phlogiston.

However, this aspect of Devitt's case points to a central problem with his view. Generally, one thinks of realism as a metaphysical position, not an empirical one. It is a question of how we understand our everyday and scientific assertions. Those assertions are the still point of the argument: they remain in place even if one is an anti-realist. The debate is not a first-order debate about the existence of electrons or dodos, but rather a second-order debate about the meaning of existence. The realist wants to assert the mind-independence of existence and the anti-realist denies the absolute split between mind and world. Therefore, simply asserting that the fact that we speak about objects is a good indicator of the mind-independent existence of objects is beside the point – it doesn't count as evidence for realism. Anti-realists also speak about objects, but they have a different reflective understanding of what that speaking amounts to. One can't annex ordinary discourse to a particular philosophical understanding in so easy a fashion. Rorty's response to Steven Weinberg comes to mind.

Weinberg tells us that all of us, in everyday life, recognise that there is a "one-to-one correspondence" between what we say about rocks and "aspects of objective reality". But ask yourself, common reader, in your capacity as everyday speaker about rocks, whether you recognise anything of the sort. If you do we philosophers would be grateful for some details. Do the subject and predicate of your sentences about rocks ("This rock is hard to move", say) stand in such a relation of correspondence? Are you sure that hard-to-moveness is really an aspect of objective reality? It's not hard for some of your neighbours to move, after all. Doesn't that make it an aspect of only subjective reality?   (Rorty 1999: 184)

Clearly Devitt's position is much more sophisticated than Weinberg's – but Rorty's point seems to hold. Whatever it is that philosophy involves, it somehow or other involves a deeper reflection on our everyday discourse, and an appeal to what seems evident in everyday discourse doesn't cut much ice for philosophers; that's not their *modus operandi*. However, even if Devitt's positive case for realism is not as overwhelming as he believes, it could well be the case that his objections to relativistic anti-realism are fatal. Let us now turn to arguments for ontological relativism and return in the final section to some specific objections, including Devitt's.

Arguments for ontological relativism

Quine

Quine's philosophy has developed over seven decades and comprises a complex system of interlocking positions. His greatness lies in the focussed development of empiricist thought, which produced important results for epistemology, philosophy of language and ontology and which defends a distinctive "desert-landscape" outlook in these areas. His austere vision has been resisted by many. Quine is of interest in this discussion because he defends relativistic views about language and ontology. His is probably the most famous use and defence of the notion of "ontological relativity". To grasp his views on ontology, we need initially to examine his attitude to knowledge and language.

Quine is an empiricist first and foremost: whatever basis there is for knowledge lies in observation. However, he eschews talk of conscious experience and trades in the idiom of stimulus and response. Further, he holds that knowledge acquisition and language acquisition go hand in hand. Instead of looking at questions about evidence for beliefs, he deals with evidence associated with linguistic practice. So the starting place in philosophy is an account of the acquisition of our verbal habits in response to our environment. Every part of this programme is controversial and open to debate. However, the reason for Quine's method and his austere naturalism lies in his attitude to the relationship between science and philosophy. A traditional account of their relationship holds that philosophy provides a foundation for science. Metaphysics, understood as a specifically philosophical enterprise, underpins all our accounts of reality. Descartes's metaphor of the tree of knowledge clearly illustrates this position, with metaphysics, as the roots, supporting the trunk (physics) and branches (other sciences). Quine rejects this traditional view because he claims that philosophy has no special resources unavailable to science. Therein lies his naturalism. Instead of epistemology underlying ontology, there is what Quine calls a reciprocal containment between them. Epistemology – the account of how we actually acquire knowledge and language – is carried on within empirical psychology, a branch of science. Thus ontology contains epistemology. However, epistemology explains the workings of science and does so from within it, immanently. In this respect, epistemology contains ontology as its subject matter. Hence the reciprocal containment. This conception of epistemology is called naturalized epistemology. Quinean naturalized epistemology deals in stimulus and response, and avoids talk of minds, beliefs and intensions. Quine's objection to these is that they play no explanatory role for a science keyed to observation and there is no other genuine option but this.

An account of the workings of language is therefore fundamental for Quine's epistemology; it explains the origins of our knowledge. His explanation of language use is a genetic account of the increasing complexity that children acquire in their linguistic practices. The basic unit of meaning is the sentence, rather than the word. The initial phrases learnt by the child – "Mama", "Milk" – responding to the environment, and gained through imitation and reinforcement, are construed as single-word sentences. Complexity enters when individuation occurs: when attempts to make a distinction between one object and another occurs in language, which involves figuring out where one object leaves off and another begins. Predication, the attribution of properties to objects, contributes a further layer of sophistication, as do the distinctions between singular and plural objects and the permutations of property attribution linked to classes. All of these refinements, although quite far down the line from the baby's simple response, are on the same behaviouristic continuum. Quine holds that it is a natural development to refer to abstract objects, construing abstract terms analogously to concrete ones. This whole linguistic edifice has built up over time and is quite haphazard. Conditions for individuating objects are not clear, and ambiguities over reference often abound. The task of science is therefore an extension of our everyday dealings with the world. It is a systematization and extension of that activity. Higher standards of rigour and clarity are demanded of scientific language, but it is not in any profound sense a different use of language – it is a continuation of everyday usage. The tool used to clarify scientific language is symbolic logic.

Quine is fond of the term "regimentation". We can regiment our language by putting it into predicate calculus. Using quantifiers and predicates, the claims we make about the world can be captured with a high degree of precision. The benefit of this is that we can also get clear about our ontology. We interpret the predicate calculus as quantifying over objects in reality. Our ontology then comprises whatever objects are required to make our best theory of the world true. We assess what is the best theory on pragmatic and instrumental grounds: the theory that best fits with observational data, and provides the most coherent and useful organization of those data. However, this is not to claim that observational data are the bedrock of Quine's system, because he accepts that observation is theory laden, that is, that there is no raw level of observation free from theory that serves as the foundation of knowledge. Talk of observation is expressed in a theoretical language, involving receptors, nerves, behaviour and so on. It is open to revision and improvement. Nevertheless, observation is accepted provisionally as the place where checks on theory can be made, even though it is itself part of that theory. This is another instance of reciprocal containment.

Quine's account of reference, and hence his account of ontology, is embedded in the use of the predicate calculus as a criterion of ontological commitment, the use of a pragmatist epistemology and the adoption of a behaviourist account of language acquisition. From this joint set of positions he holds to the doctrine of *the inscrutability of reference*. This means that there is no fact of the matter about reference. In effect, Quine is arguing that the notion of an absolute fact about reference, independent of any context, framework of ideas, or theory, is something that doesn't make any sense. This does not mean that he repudiates relative facts about reference. These are what we actually use. He makes an analogy with the notion of space. Hitherto it was thought that we needed to hold to an absolute idea of space; there was a fact of the matter embedded deep in the fabric of the universe about location in space. However, it came to be seen that a relative notion of space was all that was required. All experimentation, observation and measurement took place relative to an arbitrary set of coordinates. Quine holds that the same is true of reference; there are no absolute facts about reference, but rather relative ones. In what way, then, is reference relative?

Quine's behaviourism about language learning holds that all the evidence we have to go on is observable behaviour such as verbal behaviour and ostension (pointing). Given this basis there are many possible interpretations of any given scenario. His most famous example is of an interpreter dealing with a tribe who use a language totally unknown to him or her. They utter "gavagai" whenever there is a rabbit in the vicinity. It seems natural to suppose that it means "rabbit" for them, just as for English speakers. However, Quine draws our attention to the subtle machinery operational within language that allows us to make sense of the world around us. We individuate phenomena in our surroundings: we say x is different from or the same as y, or we say that there is a little or a lot of z about. We conceive of things as concrete or abstract, singular or plural, as masses or as individuals. We do this in ordinary language using pronouns, pluralizations, and certain alterations of vocabulary. This complex apparatus is brought to bear on the behavioural evidence. With different structurings of this apparatus, the world is thought of in different ways. Hence, relative to one way of construing the apparatus, it makes sense to say that "gavagai" equals "rabbit". However, with a different construal of the apparatus "gavagai" could mean "undetached rabbit part" or "temporal slice of rabbithood". The ontology associated with the term "gavagai" is thereby relative to the way the linguistic machinery is construed. Quine calls these construals "analytical hypotheses" and a translator between the alien language and the home language can use different analytical hypotheses to get different translations of the same utterance keyed to the same behavioural evidence. There are no absolute facts of translation available, just relative facts, relative to different analytical hypotheses. Hence there is no absolute fact of reference either, but reference is achieved also by the use of such analytical hypotheses.

This point generalizes from the case of translating foreign languages to a home language into the use of the home language itself. The ontology expressed in the home language is produced by the machinery of that language and specifically the principles of individuation operational in that language. He takes the example of the term "green". It can be used as a concrete general term (referring to green stuff) or an abstract singular term (referring to the abstract entity green). Which of these is in question is determined by the linguistic apparatus used surrounding the term. There isn't a question of the term somehow, magically, being directly linked to one or the other of these. This view of the relationship of language to reality is rejected by Quine. He calls it the myth of the museum – that words stand as labels for objects – and points out that Dewey had rejected the doctrine while Wittgenstein had still been in thrall to it, in the picture theory of meaning.

So Quine has argued that what exists is expressed in our talk about the world. Our account of what exists imposes a systematic structure on the world; we decide about individuation. Thus there is no absolute fact of the matter about questions such as "Is this x the same as that y?" There is a fact relative to a theory expressing principles of individuation. This theory can be reinterpreted into another theory and so on. But we stop at some theory and take that as basic, just like a home language when translating some foreign tongue. Our acceptance of an unquestioned basis is a central aspect of Quine's naturalism. This basis is our best current set of theories about the world. We take this as our final stopping place in explanation. It is open to revision of course, but only in a piecemeal fashion. Using Neurath's famous simile, we use our theories in the way sailors use a boat on the high seas. We can tinker with parts of it, and revise bits of it, and ultimately maybe even all of it, but at any given time we keep parts solid in order to do the work of keeping us intellectually afloat.

Quine's epistemological position is instrumentalist. Our theories about the world are instruments we use for making predictions about observations. They provide a structure in which we interpret, understand, systematize and unify our relationship to the world, rooted in our observational linkage to that world. How the world is understood emerges only in the context of these theories. We latch on to the best ones we have, take them as the "home" theories and then judge competitors from this vantage point. This attitude of privileging one group captures what Quine calls his "robust realism". We treat this theory as the truth; it is the best one we have. We have no external, superior vantage point outside theory from which we can judge the situation. Quine's realism differs then from the more traditional kind expressed above in "What is ontological relativism?" (pp. 53–63). Unlike the traditional kind, which attempts to articulate the ultimate nature of reality independent of our theorizing, Quine's realism takes on board the view that ontology is relative to theory, and specifically that reference is relative to the linguistic structures used to articulate it. Furthermore, there will always be alternative ways to present evidence, to produce a different ontology. There is no fact of the matter, outside the theory, forcing on us a particular ontological interpretation. What determine one's choice of ontology are methodological factors such as simplicity, generality, predictive power, conservativism and so on. Depending on one's choice of theory, there will be different ontologies. Ontological relativity therefore argues that ontology is theory-relative. The basic contention is that argument impinges on choice of theory; when bringing forward considerations about whether one way of construing reality is better than another, it is an argument about which theory one prefers. Whatever ontology we accept derives from whatever theory we accept. As I have shown, Quine has an instrumental view of theories – they don't reveal facts that exist at some level independent of the theory, but facts emerge internally to theories. His epistemology is empiricist, denies any genuine distinction between philosophy and science, and hence is called naturalistic. Because Quine privileges the physical sciences, especially physics, there is a hierarchy in our theories about the world. Physics, because of its scope, has a degree of cognitive superiority not held by other kinds of theories. Thus Quine doesn't have a free-for-all of theories, but privileges some. Therefore he can describe his view as robustly realistic; he takes physics at face value, given our raft-like predicament.

However there remains the tension in his work between this robust realism and the instrumentalistic and anti-realist features already discussed. Also, his adherence to physics has been criticized in some quarters as a form of dogmatic scientism; the reasons for privileging physics as he does are held to be not very strong. One way to explore these tensions and push Quine's work in a non-scientistic direction is to look at the work of Hilary Putnam.

Putnam

Hilary Putnam's (1926–) work traverses a multiplicity of areas in philosophy and has evolved over a number of distinct stages. In one sense he has always been an avowed opponent of relativism: relativism about rationality. Nevertheless, he has also advocated a form of ontological relativity, intimately linked with another form of relativism: conceptual relativity. In the following section I will first discuss his epistemological differences from Quine and then address his views about ontological relativity.

Putnam is critical of Quine's admiration of science. He doesn't repudiate scientific knowledge or propose Luddite rejections of technology, but rather claims that Quine's attitude is unbalanced: it ignores other modes of cognitive activity. Specifically he argues that reason can't be naturalized; there isn't a scientific account of rationality available in the way other phenomena can be so analysed. He argues that Quine falls foul of a general argument that arose initially against positivism. Any attempt to give an account of rationality that ties it too closely to rules or algorithms will be so restrictive as to actually outlaw the very giving of such an account; it will rule out its own formulation. The verification principle is the key example of this approach – it was so restrictive as to render its own statement either impossible or empty. As a variant of this view (labelled by Putnam a "criterial conception of rationality"), he cites the view that reason can be defined by institutionalized norms, for example, linguistic rules. How should one evaluate this claim? Well, it fails to deal with the possibility of rational critique of those norms themselves. Norms can be wrong, and presuppose a rational interpretation that cannot be dictated by other norms. Such a view of rationality removes the possibility of arguing about conceptions of rationality or produces philosophy that outlaws philosophy – a view Putnam attributes to Wittgenstein and Quine. Thus Putnam holds that rationality can't be restricted to the institutionalized norms, established, for example, by scientific activity; it must be broader than that and be capable of judging scientific activities.

This critique leads to Putnam resisting Quine's trenchant empiricism. Putnam holds that prediction of observation is too restrictive a criterion of evidence for belief; there are many more cognitive interests than prediction and so more kinds of justification than envisaged by Quine. Such narrowness derives from a residual positivism, seeking observation as a foundation – a fallible, theory-laden, sophisticatedly construed one, but nevertheless an ultimate touchstone. It also leads to an unattractive degree of eliminativism (replacing certain kinds of theory with another; for example replacing a mentalistic description, "I have a toothache" with a physicalistic description, "Brain-fibre C345 is now firing"). Too many of our common-sense beliefs end up being repudiated for not passing muster in a properly adequate scientific conception of reality. Putnam attempts to save more of our common-sense intuitions, especially those of an ethical nature. His conception of reason owes more to Kant than to empiricism. He wishes to connect the notion of rationality to that of value, and not just merely instrumental value (that it is useful to be reasonable to achieve some specified goals); there's a more intrinsic connection between reason and value. In sum, Putnam holds a post-empiricist account of epistemology and rationality, but nevertheless shares with Quine a rejection of the absolutist position about ontology. Since he can't rely on empiricist doctrines about underdetermination of theory by evidence or deploy an instrumentalist account of knowledge, he has to produce arguments against that doctrine other than Quine's.

Putnam calls what I have described above as pre-Kantian realism "metaphysical realism", saying "On this perspective the world consists of some fixed totality of mind-independent objects. There is exactly one true and complete description of 'the way the world is'" (1981: 49). One approach to showing that such a conception is incorrect is that it leads to unacceptable views about reference. For the metaphysical realist there is a fit between words and objects in reality. When we refer, we latch on to objects in a way that is independent of our interests and our knowledge. Reference connects our language with that which is independent of us. Putnam denies that this picture makes sense. The metaphysical realist has to show that there is a single relation – the correct one – between concepts and mind-independent objects in reality. Putnam holds that only a "magic theory" of reference, with perhaps "noetic rays" connecting concepts and objects, could yield the unique connection required. But no such credible theory is available. Instead, reference makes sense in the context of the employment of signs for certain purposes. Such employments occur in multiple ways and there is no unique connection between concepts and objects that stands out as the true one. Many possible connections exist and use by us is what fixes reference, not some intrinsic link of concepts to objects.

Putnam makes use of a variety of approaches to make this point. He employs examples showing that the connection isn't fixed by what goes on in one's mind. A central element in these examples is that two persons may have thoughts that are indistinguishable from each other (even to a telepath!), but still may refer to different things. So the relation isn't established by acts of meaning in our head. When we introduce environmental factors, especially causal notions, the situation doesn't change. If the meaning of a concept is established by its causal relation to the environment, there still remains the problem of what is meant by "cause" and how it differs from "cause*" (a relation of concepts to reality, close to but not quite the one supposedly picked out by "cause"). The problem is how can we be sure that the unique notion of causality required is picked out by the use of the term "cause"? If we attempt to fix the meaning of "cause" relative to "cause*" using other terms, the problem emerges again for those other terms and so on. No unique relation is picked out. He has also used a more formal argument, usually called the "model theoretic argument". This proves a theorem such that, for any language, there is always going to be more than one possible interpretation yielding alternative ontologies. He gives an example of "the cat is on the mat", showing how this can be equivalent in all possible worlds and under all operational and theoretical constraints to "the cat* is on the mat*", where "cat*" and "mat*" have a different ontological interpretation from "cat" and "mat". He then generalizes the result, showing that it is always possible to reinterpret the reference of terms while satisfying all such constraints and still produce a version different from the initial interpretation. The point common to the denial of "noetic rays", the relativizing of "cause" to "cause*" and the model theoretic argument is that there is no fact of the matter *independent of context* to reference.

That there isn't a unique fit between concepts and objects is what Putnam calls "conceptual relativity" (a phrase he explicitly distances from alethic–relativist style positions (Putnam 1987: 17)). That concepts succeed in referring is due to our use of them and not to their absolute "meanings". Basic terms such as our categories, the logical connectives and the notion of existence all acquire their meaning through the ways they are put to use by us. They don't arrive pre-processed with their meanings "built into" them. Putnam gives the example of the word "object". What is an object? That depends on what we mean by the term. Consider a world with three individuals in it, x_1, x_2 and x_3. Are there three objects there? Well, on one "natural" understanding of object, yes. However, another way of construing objects allows sums of individuals to count as objects, in which case there are then seven objects: $x_1, x_2, x_3, x_1 + x_2, x_1 + x_3, x_2 + x_3$ and $x_1 + x_2 + x_3$. There is no absolute meaning of the term "object"; it means different things as we choose to use it differently. Once such a choice is made, there is no relativity about whether there are three objects or seven objects. However, the fact is relative to the choice of concepts. Because there are facts on this account, Putnam calls his position realistic. But since the facts depend on our conceptual choices, he calls the position "internal realism" to distinguish it from the absolutist position, which he calls "external realism", or "metaphysical realism", as mentioned above (Putnam 1987: 32).

Putnam's diagnosis of the metaphysical realist position critically involves the notion of truth. Truth, on this view, is regarded as correspondence between facts and language or mind. This correspondence is absolute; it isn't altered in any way by our cognitive abilities. Hence it is possible that a belief, which to the best of our conceptual abilities in any ideal sense is judged true, could still turn out to be false. Putnam says "the sharp distinction between what really is the case and what one judges to be the case is precisely what constitutes metaphysical realism" (1981: 71). He rejects this position, however. In order to have such a correspondence between words or thoughts and mind-independent facts one needs first to have secured reference to these mind-independent facts. However, as he has argued, reference isn't achieved without making the objects in some sense mind-relative (we conceptualize them). Thus correspondence in the required sense just doesn't exist. Putnam replaces the correspondence conception of truth with an epistemic notion of truth. Truth is idealized rational acceptability. The "rational acceptability" part connects the notion of truth to our ongoing effort to make sense of reality, and the "idealized" part allows that we can always revise our judgements and accept that we were mistaken in attributing truth to some belief. As I discussed in Chapter 2, one can have an absolutist view of truth yet still have other forms of relativism. But this depends on the theory of truth you hold. Putnam holds that the correspondence theory of truth is intimately connected to metaphysical realism, so he advances an alternative epistemic theory, which allows ontological relativism. This goes right against Devitt's view that realism has no genuine connection with semantic notions – that the question of the absolute, non-relative existence of things is quite separate from how we refer to or make judgements about them. We will turn to that discussion in the next section.

Putnam's position attempts to hold two competing intuitions in tension with each other. On the one hand, there's a world independent of our creation impinging on us, and on the other, the world known to us is dependent on our point of view. This problematic reflects the Kantian backdrop to Putnam's views. Emphasizing the first intuition yields the metaphysical realist position. Emphasizing the second produces a very extreme form of relativism in which each perspective creates a different world. Putnam's gambit is to claim that both these positions are incoherent. We have looked at his argument against metaphysical realism above. His argument against extreme relativism is simply that it is self-refuting. If one claims that each perspective is equally valid, then that very view is just one among many perspectives, and it has no purchase on anyone else's position and may be safely ignored. In subsequent chapters I will return to the question about what sort of epistemological or rational constraints can coexist with ontological relativity. In the meantime, the prior question of whether ontological relativity actually makes sense, and whether it can be separated from more objectionable forms of relativism, must be addressed. It is certainly clear that the position has numerous vocal opponents who attack it with zest. These occupy the next section.

Objections to ontological relativism

Objections to ontological relativism come in two forms. One type attacks specific versions of the position, and the other consists of general arguments against any version. The literature on this is vast and growing, but I shall pick out seven objections to the view. The first three are against Putnam's position, the next against Quine and the final three are general objections that cut against all versions of ontological relativism, including those two.

1. One true picture of reality

In Putnam's characterization of the metaphysical realist position, he again and again states that it is committed to the view that there is a single true description of reality. Because there is a fixed way the world is, independent of our thoughts and interests, and because there is a relation of correspondence between that world and our thoughts, metaphysical realism must be committed to one elaborate true account of that world. So, as already noted, he says, "On this perspective the world consists of some fixed totality of mind-independent objects. There is exactly one true and complete description of 'the way the world is'" (Putnam 1981: 49).

This characterization of metaphysical realism has been rejected by those defending the view that we do have access to a mind-independent world. Those defending the claim that objects exist with identity conditions not imposed by us, do not have to say that there is just one account of those objects possible. This is the position of the sophisticated realist characterized above. The unsophisticated realist may claim that there is one fundamental true theory of the world. In so doing he or she has to defend a reductive account of theory, in which all other theories can be shown to reduce to the basic one. Such an explanatory burden is too great for most philosophers to accept (although physicalists, especially in philosophy of mind, make great claims for "future science", hoping it will deliver such an account). The sophisticated realist holds that there are many theories but one world. Against this the ontological relativist denies the usefulness or efficacy of making such a distinction, holding that the notion of the world invoked here is quite empty.

It seems, however, that this is a valid objection to part of Putnam's project. He argued that metaphysical realism was committed to a unity of theory view, and it seems clear that it isn't. As such, Putnam's case has been damaged. However, this is not a positive argument against ontological relativism. Rather it is a rebuttal of one of Putnam's arguments against metaphysical realism.

2. Truth

Putnam interprets metaphysical realism as being committed to a correspondence theory of truth. Theory corresponds to the fixed nature of reality. Putnam attacks this view of truth in a number of different ways. First, he argues that it leads to sceptical results, where truth is divorced from our epistemic capacities (Putnam 1981: Ch. 1). Such a view of truth allows scenarios such as the brain in the vat hypothesis. This hypothesis suggests that it is a genuine possibility that instead of reality being as we think it is, we really are brains in vats of nutrients connected to a super-computer that feeds us input to make us think everything is "normal". This affects all of us – there is no "normal" mad scientist monitoring the machinery – and so no possibility of establishing a reality–appearance distinction. The truth of the situation transcends all possible epistemic capacities to know it. Now Putnam rejects this sceptical position as incoherent, based on an argument about how reference works. However, he also rejects the view of truth it rests on, precisely because it divorces the nature of truth from any connection with human knowledge. Secondly, he challenges the notion of correspondence itself. Rather than denying that theory corresponds to reality, he argues that there are myriad correspondences possible. There is no question of singling out "the" relation of correspond-

ence that is supposed to explain truth. So in rejecting correspondence because, on the one hand, it leads to incoherent doctrines
and, on the other, it fails to deliver a unique account of truth,
Putnam defends a different view of truth. He analyses truth as
idealized rational acceptability. Truth is internally connected to our
epistemic practices and exists as an ideal towards which they tend.

Many objections to this view of truth have been put forward.
Michael Devitt defends the correspondence view of truth as the
correct account and rejects Putnam's epistemic theory, but also has
a more fundamental objection (Devitt 1997: 39ff.). As we have
seen, his claim is that realism has nothing to do with truth at all. The
world exists without any need of human interest or input. Truth is
part of semantics: the relatively small and insignificant part of the
world where we think about our thinking about the world. It has
nothing to do with the existence or not of that world. Therefore
realism, the position rejected by ontological relativism, has no need
of any view of truth. Devitt's maxim 2 advocates separating metaphysics from semantics.

This is a strong expression of what Putnam calls the externalist
perspective – that "the world" exists totally independently of our
cognition. Putnam can accept that the world does so exist, in the
sense that we didn't invent or construct dinosaurs, or humming-
birds or any other natural kind. Yet there is another sense in which
we do "construct" the world. This is the sense that denies the
possibility of thinking about the world "in the raw". We think via
our concepts, and these concepts have a history and a context and
shape how we think about the world. There is no mode of access to
the world other than via these concepts. The world revealed by
them is not in the control of our will; it is other than it. Devitt wants
to recruit the world revealed by our concepts as the best explanation of the way our concepts fit together. Ontological relativists
want to resist this recruitment, simply because it appears like an
appeal to what is cognitively inaccessible to us. It appeals to an
unconceptualized world to explain the conceptualized world. The
claim is that we have no meaningful access to the former and so our
discussions should remain internal to the latter. So while Putnam's
view of truth may or may not be defensible, his central contention
doesn't depend on that particular view of truth. This contention is
that we should resist appeals to the unconceptualized, the world-in-

itself. This debate turns into one about the nature of explanation and whether invocation of "inference to the best explanation" arguments can be used in a general way to support metaphysical realism, or whether such a move is redundant and non-explanatory. The debate is complex and lengthy. It suffices to make clear here that Putnam resists the realist account of explanation and his position stands or falls on the tenability of an alternative account.

3. Model theory

Putnam's technical argument against metaphysical realism derived from model theory. The claim was that there is no fact of the matter, independent of context, about reference. One could show how terms can always refer to different things, even if all constraints are adhered to; there is no absolute fixity about reference. The main opposing approach to this, arguing for fixity of reference, comes from the causal theory. Things in the world causally interact with us and appropriate causal interaction allows us to refer to them in a determinate fixed way. Putnam's response to this is to challenge how we can be sure of what "cause" means. How do we distinguish it from "cause*", which has a different reference? The problem of lack of fixity of reference attacks even our fundamental conceptual vocabulary.

There are a number of important points to be noted about Putnam's argument. The first is how precisely to interpret it. At face value it seems to be scepticism about reference; since there is no fixity about reference, there can be no genuine knowledge of it – it is not stable. Now it seems that Putnam's argument is not for this conclusion. He wants to hold on to some notion of reference. However, he does want to use his argument to attack background theories linked to reference. He holds that, if one is a metaphysical realist, problems arise for an account of reference that don't arise on his internal or anti-realist account. The metaphysical realist has to give an account of truth and reference that doesn't take into account our epistemic capacities. Putnam holds that this is essential to metaphysical realism, where truth is radically non-epistemic and therefore so also is reference. So whatever fixity of reference there is derives no support from our epistemic attitudes. Putnam maintains that there isn't any other support and so the metaphysical realist position has no viable account of reference. The second point is that Putnam himself had given, famously, a causal account of reference in his earlier work, which he hasn't disavowed, but which he seems to think unavailable to his opponents. How can this be explained?

Objections to Putnam tend to focus on this latter point. Why can't a causal theory of reference support the anti-relativist position? Various respondents to Putnam have argued that his rejection of the causal theory is not a valid move; it is too strong an argument. Its excessive strength lies in the fact that it doesn't allow an opponent even to enter the field to reply to the objection. No matter what they say, Putnam can challenge them on whether they are really asserting p, or some alternative p^*. In so doing he just stops the debate and begs the question against his opponent. So that particular argument doesn't seem to work. Furthermore, Putnam's own understanding of the causal theory of reference now seems to take it as an "internal" theory, tied into an epistemic account of truth and reference. This may well be defensible, but the argument he has given against reading it in an external or metaphysical realist fashion isn't compelling.

However, Bob Hale and Crispin Wright, for example, are nevertheless dubious about the possibility of a viable causal theory of reference. They hold that the results so far haven't been promising for an effective theory (Hale & Wright 1997: 443). So where does this leave Putnam's argument? We can distinguish the model theoretic argument itself from the reply to the causal theory. The model theoretic argument holds that reference is not fixed independently of our attitudes. If there is no viable causal response to that, one might think it still a strong claim against metaphysical realism. So ontological relativism could use it as an argument. And even if it failed, most realists are happy to concede that there is not one true theory of the world anyway, but there are multiple theories, so some sort of relativism about theory is accepted by most theorists.

Putnam's work is a clear articulation of an ontological relativism, explicitly indebted to Quine's development of ontological relativism. Yet Putnam is notoriously protean in the positions he takes. His earlier work espoused a strong realism. He then defended internal realism. In more recent work he has signalled a move again from that position, yet not back to metaphysical realism (Putnam 1999). He has offered many fruitful insights into the nature of the debate on ontological relativism. Particularly useful has been his tendency to resist scientism: to argue for rationality in a manner that doesn't identify it *simpliciter* with scientific rationality and that argued for the essential role of values in trying to make sense of the notion of fact.

4. Quine and eliminativism about meaning

Quine's version of ontological relativism seems much closer to scepticism about reference than Putnam's position. Putnam accepts that there is a fact of the matter about reference on the internalist perspective; we can fix what it is. His arguments are directed against the externalist account. Quine's position seems more extreme: there is no fact of the matter about reference, period. Reference is inscrutable because there are no facts involved. Hence no causal theory of reference could work, even of an internalist kind.

There are various interpretations of Quine available. In his recent book on relativism, Robert Kirk tends to play down Quine's ontological relativity and emphasize his robust realism (1999: Ch. 4). Kirk discusses Quine's account of rabbits. He notes that by reading the notion of "rabbit" as a posit, it seems to imply that we decide whether rabbits exist or not. Kirk thinks such a notion is absurd; we don't decide such things. We can decide to use a concept or not, but we don't decide on whether rabbits exist: "Certainly it is up to us which words or concepts we use. But that doesn't mean it is up to us whether or not those words or concepts actually apply to anything" (Kirk 1999: 169). Kirk emphasizes the Quinean dictum: "to call a posit a posit is not to patronise it" (Quine 1960: 22). Kirk explains this by saying that when we posit the existence of any entity we take it as really existent: there is no higher court of appeal. Our best theory at the moment is taken literally. There is no relativity of truth from theory to theory – we take the current evolving doctrine about the world as literally true. Kirk notes with respect to theory that

> After all, my theory – like any theory that people actually hold – is a theory about what there is! That is a logical point. Everyone is a realist about what their own theory posits, precisely because that is the point of the theory: to say what there is, what really exists. (Kirk 1999: 171)

Now it seems that this is not a logical point; indeed, it is false. A wide variety of philosophers can accept physical theory about the world, for example, yet have divergent metaphysical interpretations of what it means and how it relates to "really existing". I shall discuss this point in relation to common sense in the next objection.

If doubts can be thrown on the robust realist aspect of Quine – not least because he is the originator of ontological relativism in its current sense – can objections still be levelled against his position? Qualms arise from consideration of what else one has to accept in accepting Quine's ontological relativism. It is an assumption of his position that intensional notions are not properly constituted to yield scientific knowledge. So "meanings" – whether in the head or in language – cannot play a role in fixing reference. Paul Boghossian (1997) has recently noted some interesting points about this. Very many philosophers have accepted Quine's doubts about the analytic–synthetic distinction. Many have also accepted the view of naturalized philosophy, where a priori reasoning is eschewed in place of a more hands-on approach. Yet a great number of philosophers resist his wholesale rejection of meaning. Boghossian uses this fact to attempt to defend analyticity. His claim is that since many don't want to accept scepticism about meaning, they are forced to question again the rejection of analyticity, as Boghossian argues that there is no way to avoid meaning scepticism if you abandon the analytic–synthetic distinction in the way Quine has done.

The relevance of this point here is that Quine's account of reference will be different if intensional notions are allowed back in, as many philosophers now accept must be the case. However, whether such a move would rehabilitate realism – the position rejected by ontological relativism – is not clear. Particularly if one takes the broadly instrumentalist stance about theory held by Quine, where explanation is cashed out in terms of pragmatic considerations such as generality, simplicity and so on, one would doubt that his account could be annexed to the realist position.

5. Common sense

Devitt has argued forcefully that common-sense considerations point in favour of realism and hence against relativistic forms of anti-realism. I argued above that common sense doesn't have great weight in such matters, but the argument can be taken further. The position I defend is that common-sense views are upheld in some sense by all philosophers. However, they differ on how they are to be interpreted. Take the example "tables exist". Aristotle, Berkeley, Kant and Devitt can all agree that they do. However, what they mean by this differs dramatically. Aristotle accepts that tables exist independently of any mental constitution, yet as an artefact the metaphysical reality of the table is less than that of, say, the tree, as a natural-kind object, from which it was made. Berkeley contends that his philosophy sides with common sense in rejecting Lockean representationalism. Tables really do exist, but the metaphysical analysis of their existence denies the philosophical doctrine of mind-independent matter, which Locke advanced. Kant defends the objective existence of tables, but as phenomenal objects. They also have another noumenal reality, either as an ideal limit condition to our thoughts about tables or as a separate reality underpinning the phenomenal realm (depending on your reading of his notoriously troublesome distinction between phenomena and noumena). Devitt holds that tables exist and that this means that tokens of this common-sense type exist independently of any mental constitution. However, whatever the dialectical arguments for or against their positions, the appeal to ordinary speech to defend their position is open to all these philosophers.

Now Devitt commits himself to a naturalized position in philosophy and from that stance he could reply that I am making an illicit distinction. The distinction between common sense and philosophical discourse is denied by naturalists. As presented in talking about Quine above (pp. 63–9), there is no place for philosophy as a foundational discourse, using resources unavailable to science or common sense. Hence there is no sharp distinction between common sense and philosophy. It could be claimed that my reply relies on such a distinction.

Quine's denial of such a distinction is directed towards certain specific aspects of the philosophical side of that distinction. He rejects the view that philosophy uses special intellectual powers such as "intuition". He denies that philosophers analyse concepts in such a manner as to reveal necessary connections between them. His main target in both these rejections is the notion of necessity, which philosophers sought and which distinguished their researches from those of empirical scientists, who dealt with contingencies of the physical universe. However, one can reject *de re* necessity (that is, non-conventional, genuine metaphysical necessity), deny a linguistic or conventionalist account of the a priori, deny the analytic–synthetic distinction, as Quine does, and still defend the distinction between a claim and its philosophical interpretation. Quine's very notion of regimentation employs such a distinction. We sharpen up our common-sense claims by putting them in a notation such that we can check their ontological commitments. So we could take each one of the philosopher's articulations "there is a table" and interpret it in different ways in predicate calculus, yielding physical objects, mental objects, phenomenal objects and so on. The initial claim is philosophically inert, so to speak. It doesn't push one towards any of the competing positions on its own. So even a naturalized position has to concede the neutrality of the common-sense claim for theoretical purposes.

There is another interesting point that should be noted here. Common sense does seem, in certain respects, to be culture-specific. The particular aspect of common sense latched on to by Devitt – that objects exist in a mind-independent way – appears to be not common-sensical for large numbers of people. What I have in mind are cultures where an idealist religion pervades even the most basic forms of thought in a society. Hence, as in Hinduism, for example, when one regards the physical world as a veil of illusion, a passing mirage, where the self is essentially non-physical and where the fundamental nature of reality is non-physical, then what passes as common sense will be quite different to what passes for it in a materialist secular culture. This point is not to endorse the idealist view over the materialist, but to point out the problematic nature of the claim that common sense backs up certain metaphysical intuitions. Whose common sense?

6. No convincing examples

Nicholas Wolterstorff gives a detailed and thorough examination of the motivations for ontological relativism in his paper "Are Concept-Users World Makers?" (1987). He begins by noting the metaphor of concepts as instruments, cutting up the world. Literally taken this view would be crazy, but metaphorically it appears apt to the ontological relativist. It seems to do some work in terms of giving a relativistic account of truth and existence. He notes that holding that truth is relative is distinct from giving an analysis of truth – and wonders why Putnam, for example, spends so much time rejecting the correspondence theory and supporting the epistemic account. It is unclear whether Putnam wants to defend a relativistic account of truth and I have argued above that such a strategy is untenable. However, it still may be possible to defend the relativistic nature of ontological terms such as "existence", "fact" and so on. But Wolterstorff does not think so. By examining the meaning of "concept" in Putnam's work, in particular, he finds no support for relativistic views about ontology. He examines the possibility that a rejection of essentialism might lead to ontological relativity. Kant's anti-realism seems to derive from rejecting necessity in reality: *de re* necessity. Putnam endorses the view that necessity is relative to a description, so there is only necessity *de dicto*: relative to language, not to reality. Wolterstorff says that even if we accept this (and there are in fact good reasons not to), it still doesn't yield ontological relativism. It just says that the world is contingent – nothing yet about the relative nature of that contingent world.

He notes an important line of argument deriving from work by Nelson Goodman, also used by Putnam, which says that absolute conceptions of truth and reality lead one into contradiction. This is the claim that when we describe the world we are sometimes led into situations when we want to say contradictory things about the same facet of reality. That is, we want to (a) make statements that are true (b) make statements that genuinely conflict with each other and (c) make statements about the same thing. In order to resolve the contradiction we postulate relative descriptions reality, and say that statement 1 is relative to one description and statement 2 is relative to another description, so they don't genuinely contradict each other. So the terms involved in the descriptions are relative to the "version", "conceptual scheme", and "language-game" in which they occur. Such terms include "existence" and "fact". Wolterstorff points out the general lack of compelling examples for such a claim and furthermore says that we can find a way of resolving the problem without relativizing ontological terms. We can either argue that the initial claims are not contradictory, just different (like saying this apple is red and this apple is green – which are compatible sentences), or else that they are about different things.

Wolterstorff is correct in noting that the examples used by Putnam and Goodman are not very compelling. However, there are other examples that do seem to have somewhat more bite. Peter Strawson (1984) has perhaps provided some ideas that could be of help to ontological relativists. In his discussion of scepticism and naturalism he presented the possibility of making a relativizing move in relation to certain conflicts that arise in the area. What he means by naturalism is the disposition we have to hold certain kinds of belief and the inefficacy of reason to dislodge us from holding such beliefs. He cites as an example our beliefs that attribute moral values, personality and so on to other people. No matter how hard the sceptic attempts to make us see that there is no rational basis for such beliefs, we persist in having them. A sceptic about such would be what Strawson describes as a hard-line naturalist: one who holds that the scientific objective, impersonal view of the world is true and that these other matters are illusory. Strawson cites two areas where he thinks these debates particularly occur. One is in relation to attributing moral properties to human beings, and the other is in the attribution of secondary qualities to objects in the world. The objective scientific story tells us that colours, for example, do not really exist, but are produced by consciousness. They are not part of the ultimate furniture of the world. However, we are forced to acknowledge these qualities, since they are the way we come to know the world. Yet there seems to be a conflict: either the world has or has not these qualities. So this seems to be the kind of example that Wolterstorff was seeking. Strawson presents a scenario where two claims are made: the world has phenomenal properties, and the world does not have phenomenal properties. They are contradictory claims and they are about the same thing. Wolterstorff's response, presumably, is to claim that they are not genuinely contradictory because they are not referring to the same thing. However, in the way Strawson sets it up they are talking about the same thing: "the world". It is either the case that phenomenal properties really exist, or that they really do not. Strawson's proposed solution is to relativize the "reallys". Relative to the scheme of concepts by which we identify the world and treat phenomenal properties, there really are such properties. Relative to the impersonal scientific picture of reality, there really are not. But the central claim for Strawson is that these are not competing positions – we accept both – but we make the relativizing move to avoid contradiction. The impersonal scientific view cannot be assimilated to the personal humanistic view, or vice versa. We retain both – they are genuinely different to each other. It is possible to make judgements and claims within each domain that are objective and truth-bearing. Yet we do not reduce one domain to the other. This seems quite central to the ontological relativist position. There is no ultimate furniture of the world that can be identified in a canonical description. There are different perspectives on reality, which are irreducible to each other. A major motivation for defending such ontological relativism is to keep these perspectives available to us and to avoid the simple dichotomy of mind and world that seems to motivate much of the defence of realism – defending the view that there is a mind-independent world. It is readily assumed that mind and world make enough sense as terms to be able to set up the realist–anti-realist dichotomy and meaningfully debate it. Ontological relativists challenge that view – for them, mind and world are terms internal to the debate, gaining their meaning within the web of belief, not by stolidly standing for the "real" entities mind and world.

Strawson wants to restrict the relativizing move to the two areas discussed: moral attributes and perceptual attributes. He explicitly rejects it for mind–body relations, holding that there is no contradiction generated by distinguishing the causal realm of the biological basis of human action from the rational realm of reasons, beliefs and actions – basically following a Davidsonian line (Donald Davidson famously articulates such a position in *Essays on Actions and Events* (1980)). Indeed, in relation to the scientific impersonal view of the world, he describes himself readily as a realist. However, he differs from both the traditional scientific realist and from Quinean relativism in important ways. His acceptance of the relativizing move in the two areas discussed pushes him in some respects away from reductive scientific realism, but close to sophisticated realism. His rejection of scientism distances him from Quine. While Quine can accept as possibilities various theoretically gerrymandered ontologies, Strawson will want to put a curb on the range of possibilities available to us. The curb comes from the kind of beings we are with the cognitive capacities we have. However, significantly, for Strawson the curb is internal to reason. He is sufficiently Kantian to argue that the concepts we use and the connections between them are limited by the kinds of being we are in relation to our environment. He is wary of affirming the role of the environment, understood as unconceptualized, in fixing the application of our concepts. So he doesn't appeal to the world as readily as realists do, but neither does he accept the range of theoretical options for ontological relativism presented by Quine. There are constraints on our thought. Constraints come from both mind and world. However, there is no easy, uncontested or untheoretical account of what these things are and how the constraints work.

7. The world well lost

It is sometimes held that the world defended by ontological relativists is one with a very bizarre metaphysical nature indeed. The ontological relativist wants to hold that there are certain constraints on our thinking – we don't just invent reality. Yet they want to deny that one can appeal to the world to explain these constraints. We can't use features of the world that exist independently of thought or theory to explain the constraints on thought or theory. So the notion of the world that they seem to have is one in which there is just a brute postulation of a world in itself, which has no properties that can be used for explanatory purposes. The postulation of this world is just a fig-leaf, as Devitt puts it, to disguise the naked idealism of the position (1997: 23). Kirk describes such a world as being a kind of cosmic porridge: having a nondescript nature that is given genuine identity when put into theory (1999: 52). Goodman describes such a world as one well lost, not worth defending (1978: 20). However, rather than retreating to realism, Goodman pushes in the opposite direction to what he calls "irrealism", holding that each version (each theoretical account of reality) produces a new world. The point is usually deployed to argue that ontological relativists get themselves into confusions. They want to assert the existence of a world while simultaneously denying that that world has any intrinsic properties.

The ontological relativist wants to deny the meaningfulness of postulating intrinsic properties of the world, if it is thought that those intrinsic properties are not theoretically shaped in some sense. The realist can agree with this, but maintain a distinction between concepts (which are constructs) and the world of which they hold (which is not). They say that human products – concepts – apply to a reality that is largely not a human construct. Reality is revealed through our use of concepts, and not created by that use.

This is quite a plausible response to the ontological relativist, particularly if one adds to it the thought that there are many more objective structures in reality than the ones we pick out. We pick out features of reality relative to our interests, but there are many more features, really there, that we have not yet adverted to, or which are not yet of interest to us. So when electricity was discovered it was a feature of the real world, and not a construct of ours. When new elements are discovered they were there all along; we latch on to them. The plausibility of this line might seem less when applied to social phenomena, such as democracy, or abstract phenomena, such as numbers, or aesthetic phenomena, such as beauty. Yet for a core body of truths it seems a compelling position.

However, the basic response of the relativist is to question the easy split between world and mind, or reality and concept. Can we use the concepts of mind and world with the pre-critical insouciance required to defend the realist position? The worry of the relativist is that we cannot. The most basic concepts used to set up our ontological investigations have complex histories and inter-relationships with other concepts. The complexity of this web of relationships is short-circuited by appealing to reality itself to fix the concepts. The relativist doubts the usefulness of this move – doubts that it genuinely achieves what it sets out to do. Rather the realist privileges a certain configuration of concepts, by claiming to anchor them outside the cluster. The relativists do want to achieve discipline in their thoughts about the world. However, they think that effective discipline is an internal issue, and not something imposed from outside. Discipline in thought comes from a proper methodology – from something such as a theory of rational constraint, which is universal, rather than from supposed contact with the unconceptualized real world.

Conclusion

This has been a brief presentation of some of the central issues and arguments surrounding ontological relativism. With such a diversity of viewpoints and range of arguments it is clear that a definitive view of this currently embroiled topic is not yet possible. However, the central contention I wish to suggest is that ontological relativism is in quite a different situation to relativism about truth. In Chapter 2, relativism about truth was argued to be incoherent. In this chapter I have generally defended ontological relativism. It may turn out to be a false doctrine and the sophisticated realist may prevail. However, there clearly are significant arguments to be answered on the part of the ontological relativist and it appears to be one of the best ways that those attracted to relativistic ideas can accommodate that relativism.

Ontology, what there is, is very closely linked to epistemology, the story of how we justify our claims about what there is. In Chapter 4 I shall examine to what extent relativistic views can survive in epistemology.

4 Epistemological relativism

There are a multiplicity of different positions to which the term epistemological relativism has been applied. However, the basic idea common to all forms denies that there is a single, universal means of assessing knowledge claims that is applicable in all contexts. Many traditional epistemologists have striven to uncover the basic process, method or set of rules that allows us to hold true beliefs. Think, for example, of Descartes's attempt to find the rules for the direction of the mind, Hume's investigation into the science of mind or Kant's description of his epistemological Copernican revolution. Each philosopher attempted to articulate universal conditions for the acquisition of true beliefs. Epistemological relativism can be best expressed negatively, just as ontological relativism was expressed in Chapter 3. It rejects an absolutist conception of epistemological justification: that always and everywhere there is a sole fundamental way by which beliefs are justified.

The multiplicity of positions labelled epistemological relativism arises due to the fact that the rejection of this absolutist view yields a variety of possible positions of varying degrees of strength. Philosophers have differed greatly in the amount of relativity they allow into the epistemological process. At a level that hardly anyone rejects, there is a degree of relativity in perceptual knowledge, depending on the perceptual apparatus and location of the individual. Yet perceptual relativism is often regarded as a primitive feature of cognition, below the level at which questions about the justification of belief arises and which is compatible with an absolutist conception of justification. Indeed, in many of the great movements in the history of epistemology it was thought to be a major task to explain the compatibility of this phenomenon with the lack of relativity in true judgements made by the perceiver. Those who claimed that relativity occurred at any higher level were generally classed as sceptics, and seen as denying the possibility of objective knowledge. Appeal to the relativity of beliefs was one of the main tools of the Pyrrhonian sceptic in achieving the goal of the suspension of philosophical belief. A most significant change in contemporary epistemology has been that many philosophers now believe that relativity at the level of belief *is* possible without falling into scepticism. As I said, this view comes in a number of different strengths.

A very strong version maintains that in different cultures and different historical epochs different standards of cognitive evaluation are used, leading to radically different sets of beliefs. There is also no Archimedean position from which one can judge these different standards. One possible implication of this is that cultures and epochs are closed off from each other: the problem of incommensurability. Philosophers defending such a view face several difficulties, an obvious one being that in their own practice as philosophers they seem to make claims that transcend cultures and epochs. Opponents argue that such a position is self-refuting. Defenders need to show how it is not simply self-refuting. Richard Rorty and Steven Stich will serve as proponents of such views and, further, similar views will be treated in Chapter 5 (see "The incommensurability challenge", pp. 156–63).

A weaker form of relativism holds that developments in logic, maths and geometry have shown how a relativized notion of the a priori is possible. Traditionally it was assumed that Euclidean geometry, Aristotelian logic and Newtonian physics were unique and absolute ways of describing abstract space, logical reasoning and the physical world. In the nineteenth and twentieth centuries the development of alternative geometries, logical calculi, mathematical systems and new physics challenged that view. It seems possible that there are alternative geometries, different kinds of logical and mathematical calculi, and new ways of thinking about matter, respectively. However, this is still a limited form of relativism; there are a small number of viable possible alternatives and, most significantly, reasons are offered as to why one alternative is appropriate in a particular scenario and not in another. Thus there is an underlying conception of a means of judging appropriateness or viability. This kind of relativism therefore allows a certain kind of diversity, while requiring a more basic universal method to evaluate, manage and make rational the diversity.

Here, then, are at least two quite distinct positions to which the label "epistemological relativism" could be applied. The stronger holds that all judgements are relative to cultures and epochs and there is no universal standard at all. The weaker holds that a priori judgements are relative to different systems of a priori knowledge, but that a universal, non-relative method exists for judging the appropriateness of each relativization. So the first position, which I shall call "radical epistemological relativism" holds that all beliefs are to be relativized to incommensurable cultures or historical periods. The second position, "moderate epistemological relativism", holds that there may be alternative accounts of a priori knowledge.

But where did this epistemological relativism come from? Apart from sceptics using relativistic arguments to reject the very idea of knowledge, there have not been many defenders of relativism in the history of epistemology. The first section of this chapter tackles the question of the relation of relativism to scepticism, showing that they are different positions. Certain ways of responding to scepticism allow the possibility of epistemological relativism. Following on from that, there will be a brief survey of the currently central debates in epistemology, indicating how questions about relativism arise in them.

Scepticism and relativism

Scepticism and relativism are sometimes confused with each other. The reason for this is that one of the sceptics' main argumentative strategies is to show that there are alternatives available to what we think to be the truth. The sceptic uses this claim to hold that we don't genuinely have knowledge and we should therefore suspend judgement. The relativist also holds that there may be alternatives available, but, unlike the sceptic, maintains that more than one of the alternatives are acceptable and can constitute genuine knowledge. Hence there are underlying differences in what counts as knowledge for sceptics and relativists, which must be brought out. To do this we will initially examine typical sceptical positions, and then look at non-sceptical responses to them. It will become apparent that certain kinds of response to the sceptic open the possibility for a relativistic way of thinking about knowledge.

There have been a great number of different sceptical positions in the history of philosophy. Some ancient sceptics viewed the suspension of judgement at the heart of scepticism as a kind of ethical position. It led to a lack of dogmatism and caused the dissolution of the kinds of debate that led to religious, political and social oppression. Other philosophers have invoked hypothetical sceptics in their work to explore the nature of knowledge. These philosophers did not doubt that we have knowledge, but thought that by testing knowledge as severely as one can, one gets clearer about what counts as knowledge and greater insight results. Descartes is probably the most famous example. Other philosophers advanced genuinely sceptical positions. There are some global sceptics who hold we have no knowledge whatsoever. Others are doubtful about specific things: whether there is an external world, whether there are other minds, whether we can have any moral knowledge, whether knowledge based on pure reasoning is viable. In this section we'll focus on those who doubt the existence of the external world as the paradigmatic sceptic.

In response to this form of scepticism, one can either accept the challenge set out by the sceptical hypothesis and seek to answer it on its own terms, or else reject the legitimacy of that challenge. Therefore some philosophers looked for beliefs that were immune from doubt as the foundations of our knowledge of the external world, while others tried to explain that the demands made by the sceptic are in some sense mistaken and need not be taken seriously.

Much of traditional epistemology has been occupied with the first of these approaches. Various types of belief were proposed as candidates for sceptic-proof knowledge. For example, those beliefs that are immediately derived from perception – often called "the given" – were proposed by many as immune to doubt. The details of the nature of these beliefs varied (for example, Bertrand Russell, Moritz Schlick and C. I. Lewis gave quite different accounts). Nevertheless, what they all had in common was that empirical knowledge began with the data of the senses, that this was safe from sceptical challenge and that a further superstructure of knowledge was to be built on this firm basis. The issue, which led many to reject this position, was the tension between giving genuine content to the data of sense and simultaneously keeping it immune from doubt. The reason sense-data were immune from doubt was because they were so primitive; they were unstructured and below the level of conceptualization. Once they were given structure and conceptualized, they were no longer safe from sceptical challenge. Because of the unresolved tension, this empiricist attempt to meet the sceptic on his or her own terms failed. A different approach lay in seeking properties internal to beliefs that guaranteed their truth. Descartes's famous twin criteria of clarity and distinctness were such a version. Any belief possessing such properties could be seen to be immune to doubt. Yet, when pressed, the details of how to explain clarity and distinctness themselves, how beliefs with such properties can be used to justify other beliefs lacking them, and why, indeed, clarity and distinctness should be taken at all as marks of certainty, did not prove compelling. These empiricist and rationalist strategies are examples of how the first approach failed to achieve its objective.

In light of this lack of success, the second, indirect approach seemed more hopeful. If it could be shown that the sceptic's position was incoherent, or that it was committed to unacceptable assumptions, then it could be rejected. Various famous attempts at this have been made in the history of modern philosophy – for example, that of Kant. However, with the aim of illuminating the rise of relativistic accounts of knowledge, I wish to discuss two influential twentieth-century versions of the undermining approach to the sceptic: Wittgenstein's argument from the grammar of "know" and "doubt" and Quine's naturalistic argument.

Wittgenstein's later approach to philosophy involved a careful examination of the way we actually use language, closely observing differences of context and meaning. In the later parts of the *Philosophical Investigations* (1953), he dealt at length with topics in philosophical psychology, showing how talk of beliefs, desires, mental states and so on operates in a way quite different to talk of physical objects. In doing this he strove to show that philosophical puzzles arose from taking as similar linguistic practices that were, in fact, quite different. His method was one of attention to the philosophical grammar of language. In *On Certainty* (1969) this method was applied to epistemological topics, specifically the problem of scepticism. He deals with Moore's attempts to answer the Cartesian sceptic, holding that both the sceptic and his philosophical opponent are mistaken in fundamental ways. The most fundamental point Wittgenstein makes against the sceptic is that doubt about absolutely everything is incoherent. To even articulate a sceptical challenge, one has to know the meaning of what is said: "If you are not certain of any fact, you cannot be certain of the meaning of your words either" (Wittgenstein 1969: §114). Doubt only makes sense in the context of things already known. The kind of doubt where everything is challenged is spurious. However, Moore is incorrect in thinking that a statement such as "I know I have two hands" can serve as an argument against the sceptic. Since one cannot reasonably doubt such a statement, it doesn't make sense to say it is known either. The concepts "doubt" and "knowledge" are related to each other; where one is eradicated it makes no sense to claim the other. But why couldn't one reasonably doubt the existence of one's limbs? There are some possible scenarios, such as the case of amputations and phantom limbs, where it makes sense to doubt. However, Wittgenstein's point is that a context is required of other things taken for granted. It makes sense to doubt given the context of knowledge about amputation and phantom limbs. It doesn't make sense to doubt for no good reason: "Doesn't one need grounds for doubt?" (Wittgenstein 1969: §122).

One result of this approach to the sceptical problem is a reorientation of how philosophy itself is thought about. Wittgenstein's focussing on linguistic practices and his desire to eradicate spurious problems led to a therapeutic conception of philosophy. Philosophy doesn't present theses to be defended; it deals in platitudes presented as reminders of how we actually use language, or in casting problems in a fresh new light where they disappear. It is neither systematic nor theoretical. However, many may feel that this is in fact a return to the first form of scepticism mentioned – a method that allows one to ignore hard philosophical problems and find some kind of mental respite from them.

For such philosophers who find much of value in Wittgenstein's thought but who reject his quietism about philosophy, his rejection of philosophical scepticism is a useful prologue to more systematic work. By defusing scepticism in this way one can proceed with other questions in epistemology. Wittgenstein's approach in *On Certainty* does point in the direction of relativistic views of knowledge. Talk of language games and forms of life lend themselves to the view that standards of correctness vary from context to context. Just as Wittgenstein resisted the view that there is a single "transcendental" language game that governs all others, so some systematic philosophers after Wittgenstein have argued for a multiplicity of standards of correctness, and not a single overall dominant one. The most famous application of this idea is the so-called "Wittgensteinian Fideist" school in philosophy of religion, which claims that religious language games have their own internal criteria of correctness and that it is illegitimate to critique them using other external standards, such as those of science. This is clearly a strongly relativistic position with implications for theories of rationality, as I shall discuss in Chapter 5. In the meantime I will deal with a different response to the philosophical sceptic.

Quine's philosophy differs from Wittgenstein's philosophy in a number of ways. First, it is avowedly systematic. Secondly, it prizes the method of the physical sciences, whereas Wittgenstein thought they had no place in philosophy. Thirdly, it steers well clear of discussions of linguistic rules or ordinary linguistic practices. Yet it shares with Wittgenstein's a rejection of traditional metaphysical philosophy and it refuses to allow scepticism a dominant role in shaping the epistemological project. As we have seen in Chapter 3, Quine unites both of these themes in what he calls naturalism. Traditional philosophy believed that it had a special task in providing foundations for other disciplines, specifically the natural sciences. Part of this job was tackling scepticism. Quine rejects this role for philosophy. He doesn't see a distinction between philosophical and scientific work. The web of belief is seamless. Some work close to experience, experimenting and refining observations. Others work at a more theoretical level, enquiring into language, knowledge and our general categories of reality. It is all part of one enterprise for Quine; there are no special methods available to philosophy that aren't there for scientists. He rejects introspective knowledge, but also conceptual analysis as the special preserve of philosophers. There is no special philosophical method.

How this relates to scepticism is that scepticism is tackled using scientific means. Quine holds that this is not question-begging because the sceptical challenge arises using scientific knowledge. For example, it is precisely because the sceptic has knowledge of visual distortion from optics that he can raise the problem of the possibility of deception. The sceptical question is not mistaken, according to Quine; it is rather that the sceptical rejection of knowledge is an overreaction. We can explain how perception operates and can explain the phenomenon of deception also. One response to this Quinean view is that Quine has changed the topic of epistemology by using this approach against the sceptic. By citing scientific (psychological) evidence against the sceptic, Quine is engaging in a descriptive account of the acquisition of knowledge, but ignoring the normative question of whether such accounts are justified or truth-conducive. Therefore he has changed the subject! Quineans reply by showing that normative issues can and do arise in this naturalized context. Tracing the connections between observation sentences and theoretical sentences, showing how the former support the latter, is a way of answering the normative question.

This Quinean naturalized picture supports the ontological relativity discussed in the Chapter 3. Does it lead to epistemological relativity? In Quine it doesn't; there is a single web of belief, observation is the touchstone of objectivity and there aren't separate compartments with different sets of epistemological standards. Of course, there are many different human activities, such as writing poetry or fiction, that don't fit into this picture. Nevertheless, those that are in the business of the pursuit of truth are bound by the same epistemological standards. Beliefs are fallible and revisable, and many trade-offs between observational adequacy and theoretical simplicity can be made, but we all play by the same rules.

So both Wittgenstein and Quine have shown ways of responding to scepticism that don't take the sceptic's challenge at face value. Wittgenstein undermines the possibility of universal doubt, showing that doubt presupposes some kind of belief. Quine holds that the sceptics use of scientific information to raise the sceptical challenge allows the use of scientific information in response. However, both approaches require significant changes in the practice of philosophy. Wittgenstein's approach has led to a conception of philosophy as therapy. Quine's conception holds that there is no genuine philosophy independent of scientific knowledge. As I mentioned above in relation to Wittgensteinian therapy, there are those who use Wittgenstein's insights as a means to further more systematic philosophical goals. Likewise there are those who accept some of Quine's conclusions without wholeheartedly buying into his scientism. That they have shown different ways of resisting the sceptic's setting the agenda for epistemology has been significant for the practice of contemporary epistemology.

Scepticism and relativism differ. Relativism accepts that alternative accounts of knowledge are legitimate. Scepticism holds that the existence of alternatives blocks the possibility of knowledge. But what kinds of alternatives are being discussed here? How can knowledge be relative? To answer these questions, we now turn to some of the main issues in contemporary epistemology.

Relativism in contemporary epistemology

There are two dichotomies that set much of the agenda in contemporary epistemology. The first of these is the foundationalist–coherentist debate. Does epistemic justification require a hierarchical view of knowledge with basic, non-inferentially justified beliefs, as the foundationalist claims, or is it non-hierarchical, holistic and systematic as the coherentist claims? The second is the internalist–externalist debate. Internalists hold that in order to know, one has to know that one knows. The reasons by which a belief is justified must be accessible in principle to the subject holding that belief. Externalists deny this requirement, proposing that this makes knowing too difficult to achieve in most normal contexts. The internalist–externalist debate is sometimes also viewed as a debate between those who think that knowledge can be naturalized (externalists) and those who don't (internalists). Naturalists hold that the evaluative notions used in epistemology can be explained in terms of non-evaluative concepts – for example, that justification can be explained in terms of something like reliability. They deny a special normative realm of language that is theoretically different from the kinds of concepts used in factual scientific discourse. Non-naturalists deny this and hold to the essential difference between the normative and the factual: the former can never be derived from or constituted by the latter. So internalists tend to think of reason and rationality as non-explicable in natural, descriptive terms, whereas externalists think such an explanation is possible. Let us look at each of these debates with an eye to their relevance to epistemic relativism.

Foundationalism and coherentism

Traditional responses to the sceptic have required that some beliefs be infallible, indubitable or certain. Because of their anti-sceptical project, philosophers like Wittgenstein and Quine have created a climate in which fallible beliefs are now seen as appropriate objects of epistemological interest. Hence current debates about theories of justified belief no longer exclusively focus on achieving infallibly justified belief, but also accept fallibly justified beliefs.

Foundationalist theories of justification argue that there are basic beliefs that are non-inferentially justified. When a belief is justified, that justification is usually itself another belief, or set of beliefs. This is what is called inferential justification – where justification is passed on by inference from a prior belief. The foundationalist argues that this process must stop eventually with beliefs that are not justified in this manner. There cannot be an infinite regress of beliefs, the inferential chain cannot circle back on itself without viciousness, and it cannot stop in an unjustified belief. Hence all beliefs cannot be inferentially justified. The foundationalist argues that there are special basic beliefs that are self-justifying in some sense or other – for example, primitive perceptual beliefs that don't require further beliefs in order to be justified. Higher-level beliefs are inferentially justified by means of the basic beliefs. Thus foundationalism is characterized by the following two claims: (a) there are basic non-inferentially justified beliefs; and (b) higher-level beliefs are inferentially justified by relating them to basic beliefs – let us call this process "epistemic ascent".

How does foundationalism relate to questions about relativism? For most foundationalists, our knowledge is a unified system, in which upper-level beliefs are justified by lower-level basic beliefs. There is only one such system, because the lower-level basic beliefs are a fixed body and so there is no room for relativity of beliefs. Yet some have challenged this picture. In the *Aufbau* (Carnap 1967),

Carnap argued that there can be more than one characterization of the basic level of beliefs. He held that the basic level can be characterized in one model as comprising sense-data, which yields a phenomenalistic account of knowledge. On another model it can be characterized in a realist fashion citing beliefs about objects and properties as basic level beliefs. The former model (or constitution-system, as he calls it) is more useful for examining how empirical evidence supports theory, and the latter is more useful for clarifying the internal structures of theories. To what extent Carnap is a genuine foundationalist, however, may be open to question. The choice of lower-level beliefs is informed by the aim of the system. Hence lower-level beliefs are inferentially connected to higher-level beliefs about the structure and aims of theories, and so cannot be seen as paradigmatic basic beliefs, which deny such connections (see Friedman 1999: Ch. 6). Another way in which Carnap allows for relativistic conclusions in a foundationalist theory is by arguing that epistemic ascent can be achieved in a variety of different ways. One needs a mechanism by which basic beliefs are connected to higher-level beliefs. Such mechanisms may work in a variety of different ways, depending on the rules of transformation allowed. Relative to one set of transformation rules, the set X of higher-level beliefs is generated on the basis of set B of basic beliefs. Relative to a different set of transformation rules, the set Y of higher-level beliefs is generated from the same basic set B. Carnap holds that there is no fact of the matter as to which set of rules is correct. Rather, it is a matter of the purpose of the system of beliefs. Carnap assumes there may be a number of legitimate purposes for such a system. In the example already given, one purpose is that of stating the internal structure of a scientific theory, which might use notions of object and property in basic beliefs. Another purpose may be that of relating a scientific theory to empirical evidence and hence using reports of sense experience as basic. Carnap does hold that the latter purpose is epistemologically superior to the former, in that it makes the relevant epistemic connections clearer. One can query whether Carnap's epistemology is continuous with what most philosophers regard as epistemology and whether his notion of "rational reconstruction" is too restrictive a view of knowledge and tied to an overly deflationist view of the task of philosophy. However, the point here is that his work shows how questions about relativity can arise in a foundationalist theory – questions about whether the basis is unique and whether epistemic ascent is unique.

Coherentism rejects the structure imposed by foundationalism on epistemic justification. It denies that there are any basic beliefs and that knowledge is structured in a hierarchical fashion on the foundation of basic beliefs. The coherentist can argue in two stages. First, he or she rejects the possibility of such basic beliefs. Such an argument would show that beliefs cannot be justified without connections to another belief, or that justification requires at least two beliefs in play. Secondly, he or she argues that foundationalism rests on a mistaken structural assumption: that justification is linear in fashion. The foundationalist holds that in the chain $<s, r, q, p>$, p cannot have any role in justifying s, since vicious circularity ensues. This is, in fact, the case if justification is linear. However, the coherentist holds that justification is more complex and holistic than that. Beliefs are not justified in terms of singular relations to a preceding belief, but in multiple relations to a coherent system of beliefs. In such a context while p is justified by s, s is also justified by p, because of the complex matrix of interconnections holding all propositions in place in the system.

Coherence has to be explicated as more than mere lack of contradiction. A system with no genuine connections between the beliefs at all lacks contradiction. Also a system that contains "p" and "it is extremely unlikely that p" is not, strictly speaking, contradictory, but may be quite unstable. Hence making sense of the relations that constitute coherentist justification will involve issues like explanatory support and evidential support, and perhaps issues about probability and confirmation too. Quine and Neurath's image of a system of beliefs as a boat at sea is one of the best images of the coherentist position. As discussed above (p. 68), the boat holds together and performs its function by virtue of its structural integrity. There is no foundational part. Also, each part can be altered or removed provided the right alterations are made elsewhere in the system to ensure that it is still a stable system.

Now, a standard objection to coherentist accounts of justification is germane to questions about relativism. If membership of a coherent system suffices to justify a belief, how do you cope with different such systems? There seems to be an endless supply of hypothetical coherent systems that supply justification to potentially contradictory statements. Such a vista is usually seen as a major problem for coherentists, since it leads to radical relativism. This is due to the lack of any principled way of distinguishing systems because coherence is an internal feature of belief systems. Responding to this, coherentists typically argue for the existence of just one system, assembling all our beliefs into a unified body. Such a view led to the unified science movement in logical positivism (a similar view has recently been endorsed by Edward O. Wilson's *Consilience* (1998)). Sometimes transcendental arguments have been used to achieve this uniqueness, arguing from the general nature of belief to the uniqueness of the system of beliefs. Other coherentists attempt to use observation as a way of picking out the unique system. It is a moot point to what extent this latter group are still coherentists, or have indeed moved to a position that is a fusion of elements of foundationalism and coherentism (e.g. Susan Haack's "foundherentism" – see Haack 1993).

If one maintains that there is just one system of beliefs, then one is clearly non-relativistic about epistemic justification. On the other hand, if one allows a myriad of possible systems, then one falls into extreme relativism. However, there may be a more moderate position where a limited number of alternative systems of knowledge were possible. On a stronger version, these would be globally alternative; there would be many complete and separate systems. On a weaker version they would be distinct local subgroups within a single system. Radical relativism, as I shall discuss below, is a coherentist model that ends up with multiple systems and no overall curbs on the proliferation of systems. Moderate relativism would come out as holding to local subsystems within a global system. So relativism about justification is a possibility in both foundationalist and coherentist theories. However, the accounts discussed in the following sections ("Radical epistemological relativism", pp. 106–117 and "Relativism about the a priori", pp. 117–29) both have coherentist structure.

Internalism and externalism

Most of the epistemological tradition has been internalist, with externalism emerging as a genuine option only in the twentieth century. The best way to clarify this distinction is by considering another one: that between knowledge and justification. Knowledge has been traditionally defined as justified true belief. However, due to certain counter-examples to it published by Edmund Gettier in 1963, the definition had to be refined and no single agreed-on version now exists, but an example of a revised version is "knowledge is undefeatedly justified true belief". (Gettier (1963) came up with possible situations in which a target belief might be both true and justified, but still intuitively we would not call it knowledge.) The extra element of undefeatedness attempts to rule out the counter-examples. However, the relevant issue here is that on all accounts of it, knowledge entails truth; one can't know something false. Justification, on the other hand, is the account of the reason one has for a belief: the story about how one can hold the belief in a warranted manner. Crucially, one may be justified in holding a false belief. Justification is understood from the subject's point of view; it doesn't entail truth.

Internalism is the position that says that the reasons one has for a belief, its justification, must be in some sense available to the knowing subject. If one has a belief, and the reason why it is acceptable for one to hold that belief is not knowable to the person in question, then there is no justification. Externalism holds that it is possible for a person to have a justified belief without having access to the reason for it. For example, children, animals and, perhaps, inarticulate people would be denied knowledge on the internalist conception, since they can't express (and aren't aware of) the reason for their belief. This view seems too stringent to the externalist, who can explain such cases by, for example, appeal to the use of a process that reliably produces truths. One can use perception to acquire beliefs, and the very use of such a reliable method ensures that the belief is a true belief. Hence we can attribute knowledge to those who cannot articulate reasons for their quite primitive beliefs – such as perceptual grasp of regular objects in the immediate environs. The externalist connects beliefs quite directly to truth by invoking a process or mechanism that produces a high ratio of true beliefs. The internalist, on the other hand, does not have such a strong connection to truth in dealing with questions of justification.

At first, externalist accounts of knowledge seem less open to relativism than internalist accounts. This is because externalism emphasizes the link to truth, and truth, as argued above, is absolute. Since truth isn't relative, accounts of knowledge that tie knowledge to reliably acquiring truth can't be relative either. However, some externalists have produced accounts of knowledge with relativistic aspects to them. Alvin Goldman is well known for his reliabilist account of knowledge in *Epistemology and Cognition* (1986). Such an account uses the notion of a system of rules for the justification of belief – Goldman calls them "J-rules". These rules provide a framework within which it can be established whether a belief is justified or not. The rules are not to be understood as actually consciously guiding the cognizer's thought processes, but rather can be applied from without to give an objective judgement as to whether the beliefs are justified or not. What is also required is a criterion of rightness to determine which framework of rules actually succeeds in capturing the required notion of justification. The framework establishes what counts as justification, and the criterion establishes the framework. Genuinely epistemic terms like "justification" occur in the context of the framework, while the criterion, on the other hand, attempts to set up the framework without using epistemic terms, using purely factual or descriptive terms. As Goldman says

> We examine what rule systems would likely be generated by each candidate criterion. We reflect on implications of these rule systems for particular judgements of justifiedness and unjustifiedness. We then see whether these judgements accord with our pretheoretic intuitions. (Goldman 1986: 66)

The criterion he settles on is reliability – that the framework produces a sufficiently high ratio of true beliefs. However there may be a variety of such frameworks compatible with this criterion: "there may be different systems of J-rules, each of which would be right, as judged by a single criterion of rightness" (*ibid.*: 70). Goldman explicitly holds that this is not to say that there may be different frameworks for different groups of people, cultures or societies, but rather that every person may have the possibility of recourse to different frameworks of rules. His analogy is with justice. While there may be a single criterion of what counts as justice, this is compatible with a plurality of different social institutions, each of which is just. So there is scope for limited relativism in externalist accounts of knowledge and justification.

Internalist accounts of justification seem more amenable to relativism than externalist accounts. Because it is from the point of view of the subject, internalist justification allows for a variety of perspectives. Internalist accounts of justification aren't constrained by the target belief having to be true. For example, I am justified in believing that there is a lecture by an eminent philosopher happening in a nearby room, because posters had advertised it, colleagues and students have spoken to me about it and I have seen a tweed-suited gentleman being ushered in by people I know. All of these elements – perception, testimony, coherence with prior beliefs – come together to give an impressive justification for the belief that a lecture is being given by a visiting academic. However, it turns out to be a hoax engineered by the student philosophy society during rag week and the "visitor" turns into a singing telegram announcing the hoax and denouncing the credulity of the philosophy department. My justification was still acceptable, as there was no way I could have known otherwise. The students, however, were also justified in believing the negation of my belief, since they had more information than I had. And their belief was true, so they had knowledge while I did not. But there were two valid justifications pointing to contrary beliefs. Such considerations have led epistemologists to think that context must play an important part in thinking about justification and knowledge. Rather than saying "S is justified in believing P", we might have to say "S is justified in believing P relative to context C". In this way, ascriptions of justification to subjects will be relativized to contexts. But clearly there will be degrees of this. If there are a multiplicity of contexts, with few or no constraints on what counts as acceptable or not, there is a radical relativism. If, however, there are significant constraints on what counts as an acceptable context, the degree of relativism is greatly lessened. Recent work on contextualism has investigated this issue.

Contextualism

If there is a situation where someone can say "S knows that P" and at the same time some other person can say "S does not know that

P", it seems that one of them must be wrong, as otherwise a contradiction will ensue. However, contextualists claim that this situation often does hold and without contradiction. This is because "to know" means different things in different contexts. Other words are similarly contextually sensitive – for example, "empty" or "flat". A warehouse is empty to the person who wishes to store things in it, but not empty to the microbiologist or the physicist who needs a vacuum chamber. A road can be flat to those used to third-world tracks, but intolerably bumpy to those used to smooth motorways. Different standards are used to apply the term in each case. Contextualists claim that knowledge is similarly context sensitive and knowledge ascriptions are made relative to some set of standards.

For example, I can say that Mary knows her children are in the garden, given that she checked five minutes ago and has no reason to think otherwise. However, if I now have the knowledge that a child kidnapper is lurking in the neighbourhood, I revise the standards I use to judge whether Mary knows the whereabouts of her children and am now reluctant to affirm that Mary knows that her children are in the garden. This example brings out two further aspects of the contextualists' position. One can speak of the subject's context (in this case Mary) and the ascriber's context (in this case me). The standards of knowledge in question may vary with both (subject's and ascriber's) contexts. Mary can legitimately use certain standards in the context of her situation, whereas I legitimately use different standards in my different context. Both of us have legitimate claims to "knowledge", but our contexts differ. Crucially, there is no epistemic blame attached to Mary in her context; she is not at fault for not considering the possibility of a deranged kidnapper being in the vicinity, since she has no good reason to consider this possibility. However, because I have good reason to believe that there is one, I have to factor that in, and I would be at fault if I did not.

But what factors influence our choice of standards? Mark Heller suggests that "Our standards change in accordance with our interests, in accordance with the demands of our conversational partners, and in accordance with which facts or possibilities are most salient to us" (1999). An important point to note is that while knowledge ascriptions are contextually sensitive in such ways, this does not lead to extreme relativism – to a kind of subjectivism where idiosyncratic contexts and interests hold sway. Relative to a given context, set of interests and range of possibilities, there is an objective answer about whether "S knows P". It is similar to the situation with indexicals – using terms like "I" or "this". These only make sense in a given context, but given that context one can establish absolute truth-claims with them.

A further aspect of contextualism, which cuts against a strongly relativistic reading of the position, is that general epistemic standards hold in place and govern the more localized contextual aspects. The exact details of what these might be differ from theorist to theorist, but certain general tenets seem to hold. These will be addressed in Chapter 5, articulated as a core theory of rationality. But first we will turn to philosophers who emphasize the local contextualized aspects of knowledge to the extent that they affirm radical epistemological relativism.

Radical epistemological relativism

Richard Rorty

Richard Rorty is generally regarded as a paradigmatic proponent of relativistic ideas. However, this widespread view of his work is *prima facie* rendered problematical by the fact that in a number of different places in his published works he has attacked the idea of relativism, arguing that it is an incoherent position and that one is much better off without it. On closer inspection the problem comes out as being terminological; what he means by relativism and what is generally held as such come out as being different things, as I shall try to show below.

His work began with his earlier analytical philosophy of mind, where he accepted the presuppositions and contexts of the analytical tradition. However, in *Philosophy and the Mirror of Nature* (1980) he carried out a radical critique of that tradition. He attempted to show the historical story to a set of assumptions about knowledge, mind and world, which were essential to making sense of enquiry within that tradition. His intellectual mentors in this project were Wittgenstein, who taught him how to spot deep-rooted prejudices, and intellectual blind-spots in thinking, Heidegger, who showed the importance of tradition and historical research to contemporary inquiry, and Dewey, who gave a social and political rationale for the project of such a historically attuned intellectual therapy.

Rorty's central contention in *Philosophy and the Mirror of Nature* is that a certain picture held philosophy captive in the modern period. This picture showed that mind was essentially immaterial, that knowledge consisted in establishing a set of privileged representations in the mind of a non-mental reality and that truth was correspondence between the representations and the non-mental reality. In such a picture, epistemology plays a central place in philosophy and indeed in culture in general. It articulates in detail the elements of this picture and in so doing provides a foundation for all other intellectual enterprises. Rorty argues that this picture emerges in a particular historical epoch, it has a history, it is not one shared by ancient and medieval philosophers and so it cannot be characterized as a timeless intuition shared by all reflective individuals. Indeed, he challenges the view that philosophy engages with a stable set of "great questions" that transcend historical epochs. His way of making this general point is to work through this specific example about mind and world. A more localized point is that contemporary analytical philosophy, while criticizing certain tactical elements of the seventeenth-century picture, still holds to the general strategy. While the mind might now be construed in a physicalistic fashion, the task of philosophy as the arbiter of objectivity and the provider of the foundations of culture still remains. One contemporary manifestation of this is the drive to establish a theory of reference as the best way of explaining the mind–world connection. In so doing, philosophy of language allies with epistemology to yield foundations for culture at large.

Rorty uses the work of Quine, Sellars and Davidson to perform an immanent critique of the analytic tradition. Quine's attack on the analytic–synthetic distinction, Sellars's criticism of the myth of the given and Davidson's rejection of correspondence all provide Rorty with ways of dismantling philosophy's claim to be a foundational discipline. Quine demolished the logical positivist's view of philosophy as the analysis of meanings, Sellars undermined empiricism and Davidson showed a way beyond traditional realist–idealist controversies. By working through the details of each of these problems, Rorty believes that philosophy is best seen not as a process of answering traditional questions, but rather as an exercise in imagination, in providing novel scenarios for intellectual development. He finds similar tendencies in contemporary continental philosophy. Gadamer gives him the idea that the goal of thinking is *Bildung* (education, self-formation) rather than knowledge. Rorty calls this style of thinking "edification": "the project of finding new, better, more interesting, more fruitful ways of speaking" (Rorty 1980: 360). Philosophers tend to be either systematic or edifying. The systematic philosophers are those who offer arguments and have their eye on eternity. The edifying are parasitic; they demolish systematic pretensions and have their eye on current preoccupations of the age. In work subsequent to *Philosophy and the Mirror of Nature*, Rorty has practised edifying philosophy. He has dialogues with a wide variety of cultural figures, from Heidegger, Derrida and Habermas, through Nabokov and Orwell, to Putnam, Searle and Dennett. His writing has an audience far beyond traditional philosophy and exhibits a literary elegance and moral fervour little seen in contemporary analytical writing.

Rorty's edifying philosophy seems to commit one to very strong relativism indeed. It denies a strong conception of external reality in rejecting the notion of objectivity as reference to a mind-independent reality. It rejects the view that some forms of enquiry depict nature as it is in itself. It proposes a conversational model of enquiry, where we learn to talk in more creative ways. It views truth as simply being able to hold one's view against all comers. It is historicist, denying perennial questions, and anti-essentialist in rejecting human nature (or indeed any other fixed nature). So how much more relativist can one get? It regards epistemological enquiry as wrong-headed; the search for objective knowledge is replaced by the creation of novel descriptions and vocabularies.

Putting these views into an idiom rather different from that used by Rorty, it seems he is committed to the following theses:

1. Ontology is relative.
2. Truth is not correspondence.
3. Enquiry is culturally and historically contextualized in that:
   - questions are local to historical periods; there are no perennial questions
   - the standards of enquiry are local to societies; there are no universal standards.

So far in this book I have accepted theses 1 and 2 and offered arguments from Putnam and Quine supporting them. Rorty believes that thesis 3 goes with them. Yet it doesn't automatically follow, or at least neither Putnam nor Quine accepts it. That is, one can accept ontological relativity and the rejection of correspondence truth, while not buying into relativism about the standards of cognitive evaluation – that is, holding that they are historically or culturally relative. What reasons does Rorty offer for the view that they are, and is his case convincing?

Rorty distinguishes between the objective tendency in philosophy and the tendency towards solidarity. The objective strand seeks to locate human self-knowledge and self-understanding in relation to ahistorical standards, and fits neatly with the systematic style of philosophy mentioned above. The other pursues the process of self-reflection in relation to community, which is construed in a contingent, historical manner. Rorty believes that his detailed examination of the seventeenth-century picture of mind and world has shown the untenability of the former style of philosophy; the notion that there are essences to mind, reality and truth rests on metaphors that should be cast aside. He says

> the best argument we partisans of solidarity have against the realistic partisans of objectivity is Nietzsche's argument that the traditional Western metaphysico-epistemological way of firming up our habits simply isn't working anymore.
>
> (Rorty 1991: 47)

Using the terminology of Chapter 3, he denies metaphysical realism (ontological universalism) and truth as correspondence, holding that in the demise of these one is forced into "solidarity". But what exactly is "solidarity"? It is the style of thinking best exemplified by modern Western liberal democracies. It carries on the ideals of the Enlightenment and strives to maintain personal, intellectual and moral freedoms and to create society on a humane model.

Rorty's central point is that this project does not require philosophical underpinning. It is a broad movement, with strands in politics, the arts, social studies, literature, urban planning and so on. All of these strands operate in a contingent, historically situated way and it is neither necessary nor sufficient for them that they have a philosophical underpinning. He therefore says that the proponent of solidarity is not in the business of offering a new metaphysics or epistemology; it is precisely the questioning of the need for such things that distinguishes such an intellectual.

Due to this profound rejection of the traditional philosophical project, Rorty can be dismissive of relativism. He understands the very idea of relativism as being inextricably entangled in misguided philosophical baggage. "Not having any epistemology *a fortiori* he [the friend of solidarity] doesn't have a relativist one" (Rorty 1991: 38). In one sense of relativism, the very idea is obviously misguided:

> "Relativism" is the view that every belief on a certain topic, or perhaps about any topic, is as good as any other. No one holds this view . . . If there were any relativists, they would of course be easy to refute. One would merely use some version of the self-referential argument used by Socrates against Protagoras.
>
> (Rorty 1982: 166–7)

Rorty holds that relativism is a product of the misguided realist position. Because the realist can't cope with the idea of being fully contingently inside a particular historical tradition and ethnocentrically thinking from within that tradition, the realist creates the illusory position of standing back from different traditions and viewing them as being ungrounded philosophically and hence as being epistemically relative. On the contrary, the friend of solidarity doesn't stand back, but enthusiastically endorses his or her own position, immanently, as it were. There's no question of the disinterested standing back required by relativism. Hence relativism is alien to Rorty's self-understanding.

Nevertheless, given that there is a great deal of cognitive disagreement in the world and that Western liberal democrats are rare enough (even in Western liberal democracies) there is something quite odd about Rorty's position. It has certain features akin to the position in philosophy of religion known as fideism. That is, one's beliefs, held sufficiently firmly, don't require rational justification. They provide the context within which we make sense of the world and are not up for grabs themselves (although Rorty's beliefs differ from the fideist's fixed faith in being mutable and responsive to a changing environment). However, the chief problem for such fideists is other fideists who hold contrary ideas. A stand-off occurs. One of the attractions of some conception of reason is to provide a neutral language in which communication and debate can carry on. Part of the task of philosophy is to investigate and articulate such a conception.

Now, Rorty deplores the idea of ahistorical reason. Partly this is due to excesses in the use of such an idea: that reason could be codified in a series of rules and that debates could be solved by appeal to such rules. Rorty rightly holds that philosophy is a kind of exchange that is characterized precisely by not following such algorithmic practices. Partly it is due to his belief that the underpinnings of such an idea – ontological absolutism and truth as correspondence – are gone. Yet he seems prematurely defeatist in not allowing any theoretical characterization of rationality that might help mediate debates between those whose views are radically opposed. Can a conception of rationality be established that doesn't rely on the rejected notions of ontology and truth, but on some other ideas? Some notion of intersubjectivity that could facilitate such a conception of rationality and truth could still be kept in the picture on some theory other than the correspondence theory, and advanced as a claim of analytical epistemology. I shall try to sketch such a conception in Chapter 5. But in the meantime here are some considerations that might give friends of solidarity pause. Rorty's characterization of Nietzsche and Loyola as being "crazy", as being outside the realm of those who are regarded as part of the "people like us" group, should alert one to the sectarian dangers of ethnocentrism (Rorty 1991: 187). It is hard to see how one can genuinely carry out a fruitful dialogue without appeal to a hard-won space where alternative views are sympathetically examined. Rorty supports the idea of such a process, but without needing any special appeal to philosophy. However, if one accepted that a task for philosophy was to facilitate such encounters by the very task of clarifying, articulating and defending such notions as "rationality", then much of what is radical (and what many find unacceptable) in Rorty's position begins to disappear. Just as he had accused traditional philosophers of setting up a privileged role for philosophy, with absurd pretensions, so, too, does he set out a special position, distinctive in its refusal to allow philosophy any particular role. In this, Rorty's view is just too extreme. Because one model of ontology, truth, rationality, epistemology and so on fails, does not mean the whole philosophical enterprise (whatever that is!) also fails. A fallible, historically, politically and scientifically attuned reflection on questions of meaning, truth, reason and so on *is* philosophy, and is what people like Habermas, McDowell, Putnam and Quine, to mention just a few, are doing. One may disagree with them (indeed being part of the philosopher's club seems to entail disagreeing), but it reflects too much of an all-or-nothing style of thinking to reject epistemology and metaphysics because certain versions of it haven't worked, and instead plump for sociopolitical analyses of "truth", "rationality", "warrant" and so on. As Searle once remarked *a propos* Wittgenstein, just because his early theories of philosophy failed, he concluded that all philosophy was doomed to fail. In some forms of anti-philosophy one can find an enormous philosophical hubris lurking just beneath the surface. Rorty has done a great service in his criticism of the analytical tradition, forcing it to be more self-aware. However, self-criticism doesn't always mean self-annihilation, as Rorty seems to think in this case.

I now wish to turn to another proponent of a strong form of epistemological relativism – a philosopher who appeals to insights from psychology to do so.

Stephen Stich

In common with Rorty, and, indeed, with Putnam and Quine, Stich claims to be strongly influenced by the pragmatist tradition (Stich 1990). The relativism he defends is similar in certain respects to that of Rorty, but his means of defending it are different. His approach owes more to cognitive science and empirical psychology than Rorty's and, indeed, he conceives his work on rationality and relativism as firmly rooted within an interdisciplinary scientific approach to cognition. Nevertheless, the epistemological relativism resulting from this approach is at least as radical as that of Rorty. Stich denies that there is any real role for epistemology, conceived of as establishing general norms of reasoning or acquiring knowledge. He believes that there are no such universal norms. He denies that truth is the goal of cognition. Neither can evolutionary advantage serve as an explanation for cognition. There are a potential multiplicity of different cognitive processes, geared towards different goals, and no one dominates within the multiplicity.

The logic of his position appears to be that by excluding traditional ways of anchoring the epistemological project he opens the way for a new kind of project that is relativism-friendly. So let us look at his negative evaluation of each one of these aforementioned ways of grounding the epistemological project before turning to his own positive position.

He rejects the view, associated with Nelson Goodman, that epistemology is the task of achieving reflective equilibrium between our pre-theoretical intuitions and our normative principles. John Rawls made such a procedure famous in his *A Theory of Justice*, but its earlier manifestation was in epistemology, where the theorist's job was that of getting intuitions and principles to cohere with each other in a systematic way. Justification is then explicated in terms of a set of rules that pass this reflective equilibrium test. Stich rejects this approach on empirical grounds. Principles can pass the reflective equilibrium test that are clearly not acceptable – for example, various kinds of probabilistic fallacy. A subject can adopt a principle (for example, that the number of heads consecutively flipped in a coin-tossing increases the probability of a tail appearing) and this principle coheres with the subject's intuitions, but it's just not acceptable. Hence reflective equilibrium doesn't actually connect with our actual cognitive practices. Yet in objecting in this manner Stich is committed to the view that there are standards and that fallacies can be seen as such – an explanatory debt he has to redeem in his positive account.

However, he further attacks the method of reflective equilibrium by arguing that it is question-begging in an unacceptable way. Suppose one is faced with a situation of cognitive diversity – for example, people use inference rules in an apparently strange way. We weigh up their inference rules against our intuitions about how they should be. Surprise, surprise – they don't match and we think the situation epistemologically suspect. Stich maintains that this says nothing at all against the deviant inferrers, since they may well have different intuitions to ours and their inference practices may accord well with their intuitions. Reflective equilibrium merely balances intuitions with practices; it cannot mediate between conflicting intuitions and crucially cannot rule out the possibility of alternative epistemic practices.

He rejects a virtually universally held view in the philosophical tradition: that truth is the goal of cognitive processes. He does this by looking for a plausible account of the relationship of mind to world and specifically how psychological states, such as beliefs, come to have semantic properties (true/false). On examining plausible candidates for such an account, he then queries whether this is why people value having true beliefs. His answer is no. He explains this by pointing out that "truth" doesn't pick out any specific relation between beliefs and entities that might carry semantic value (e.g. propositions). There are multiple possible mappings of the relations between the psychological states and the semantic bearers of truth values. The one ordinarily called "truth" is just one among a multitude of other relations, which could be "truth*", "truth**" and so on. Nothing special about "truth" is revealed in this procedure and so nothing special turns on that notion for us. Hence he claims, provocatively, that we don't care whether our beliefs are true or not.

The third view rejected is that a single model of cognition affords us evolutionary advantage. A number of theorists hold that it does. For example, for Quine, "creatures inveterately wrong in their inductions have a pathetic but praiseworthy tendency to die out before reproducing their kind" (1969: 126). Stich carries out a detailed discussion as to why there doesn't have to be a single model. There are a number of elements in play in any cognitive situation; particularly relevant are those concerning resources available to the subject (such as body mass, power of memory, perceptual sensitivity, physical resilience, etc.). Even if natural selection tends to optimize results – that is, provide a system that gives us advantage in surviving and reproducing – such a cognitive system is only one element in a greater situation that always involves complex trade-offs. For example, there's a tension between providing a system that rarely goes wrong but acquires little information, and one that generates lots of information but is unreliable. So in a poisonous environment it would be important for a creature to have a reliable system that identifies just a small section of available foodstuffs but guarantees its safety. In a non-poisonous environment, a system that identifies a large range of foodstuffs, but goes wrong in also selecting non-foodstuffs (but not poisonous ones) is advantageous. Stich's point is that such trade-offs are always part of an evolutionary situation, and they become very complex when you factor in issues such as predators, parasites and pathogens, which are also adapted to compete with the subject. In such a situation it becomes virtually impossible to state in any convincing manner what counts in general as an optimal system.

With these three ways of explaining cognition out of the way, Stich offers a different approach, which he labels the "pragmatic" approach. Cognitive processes are not for providing truths, but rather are tools for achieving goals. These goals can be as varied as the things people find valuable. Relativism arises in two ways on this conception. First, there may be a variety of different goals, and there may be a variety of different cognitive systems geared towards achieving them. Secondly, depending on the context and environment, what in fact are the same systems may in fact produce different results. Stich accepts that some of the goals may be biologically predisposed, such as health, happiness and the well-being of offspring. Some others may be culturally established and not universal, such as diverse forms of religious goals, whereas some may still be quite idiosyncratic (the pursuit of excellence in analytical philosophy?). Different cognitive systems will be appropriate to each of these. Also, in varying contexts the systems may produce different results.

Now what can be made of all this? Part of the problem with Stich's approach is that it is so self-consciously radical that it takes great pleasure in advancing counter-intuitive results without adequate defence. His attack on the evolutionary story is quite compelling, but those on truth and reflective equilibrium are rather less plausible. His attack on truth as the goal of enquiry is open to the charge that he is confusing truth with theories of truth. People really care about truth, but may not care so much about theories of truth. Think of the analogy with money; while people may not care much about whether one has a theory of intrinsic value, or a transfer theory or whatever to give an explanation of the phenomenon, it is patently false to infer from that that people do not care about money. Likewise with truth. People care about the pre-theoretic phenomenon "truth", despite the varying theoretical explanations of it. Stich's appeal to notions of "truth*" and "truth**" seems to deal more with theoretical accounts of what everyone can accept at a pre-theoretical level as "truth", captured minimally in the Tarski schema.

In attacking reflective equilibrium approaches to explaining cognition, Stich uses the example of an individual's bringing to agreement of principles and intuitions. He acknowledges that this can be challenged by the idea of experts in an area, whose reflective equilibrium trumps the uninformed individual and provides the normative standards in the area. Stich's response to this challenge is to query how experts can be identified in a non-question-begging way. Stich makes the situation problematical for the analytic episte-mologist by demanding high standards of evidence, noting that their empirical assumptions may turn out false, or that they can't guarantee that "nutty sets of rules" won't be endorsed by a commu-nity. Yet this is to deploy traditional sceptical techniques: demand-ing infallibility in an area and declaring no knowledge present when the demand is not met. One can come up with fallible results using the reflective equilibrium method, which is fine as long as you don't hanker after deeper infallible goals. Ironically, in his desire to estab-lish radical cognitive diversity and revolutionize cognitive studies, Stich has to use very conservative arguments against his opponents.

However, his other attack on reflective equilibrium takes us to the heart of the problem of epistemological relativism. Can there be radically alternative intuitions about what counts as knowledge, correct inference, induction and so on? This is the topic that will be discussed in Chapter 5, under the heading "Relativism about rationality". However, before doing that I wish to comment on a specific troublesome strategy used by epistemological relativists, and then discuss a final kind of epistemological relativism.

What is common to both Stich and Rorty is a tendency to set up dichotomies as if they were mutually exclusive and jointly exhaus-tive of the options. Rorty rejects a traditional conception of philosophy as seeking to find objectivity in the transcendent and non-human. Stich rejects more recent attempts to do the same in the scientific world. Both have quite compelling cases to make against their opponents. However, they then both leap to a position that is supposed to be the only alternative to the rejected position. Rorty speaks of intersubjective agreement as the new objectivity, and Stich talks of achieving diverse cognitive goals. The implication in both cases is that while these are meaningful locutions it is a retreat to the rejected conception of philosophy to seek further explanation as to why certain goals and methods are preferable to others and for what reasons communities come to agreement over issues. In fact, both are largely right in their rejection of traditional ways of explaining objectivity and cognitive success, but fall foul of explaining how objectivity emerges in the new "conversational" context, other than saying that it generally does. An important task for philosophers who are persuaded of the failure of some of these traditional projects, but who are dissatisfied by the skimpiness of explanation of how objectivity as intersubjectivity is supposed to work, is to try to establish how it does. A beginning for such a project is to look at a priori knowledge. This had served as a paradigm of ultra-objective knowledge for millennia, but in the past century or so radical developments in epistemology led to a proliferation of relativistic doctrines about it. In looking at these developments, a way can perhaps be seen of explaining how objectivity as intersubjectivity can be cashed out in a more developed way, allowing for relativism yet also allowing for epistemic responsibility.

Relativism about the a priori

A priori knowledge has long served as a model of absolute and universal knowledge. It consists of beliefs that are not altered by the vagaries of experience and that therefore seem to be the most strongly justified beliefs we could have. Hence they appear unlikely candidates for relativistic thought. Notwithstanding this, a plausible account of the a priori exists that allows for relativity about such beliefs. To discuss it, I shall initially give a sharper characterization of the a priori and the kinds of knowledge involved therein. Then I shall present a classical explanation of the a priori and contrast that with a radically relativistic explanation. Both such accounts have shortcomings and one reaction to those shortcomings is to be sceptical about the a priori *in toto*. I shall reject such scepticism and articulate the account of the a priori that takes a middle course between the classical and the radically relativistic, allowing a limited relativism about the a priori.

The very idea of the a priori concerns the justification of belief. If a belief can be justified without requiring experiential input, then it is characterized as an a priori belief. It is an open question how such justification may occur and various theories have been offered – for example, by proposing special non-empirical powers of the mind, or by relying on the resources of language and meaning, or by appeal to the properties of non-empirical abstract entities. Traditionally, a priori beliefs were also held to be necessary: they *had* to be true – there is no possible world in which they are false. Yet it is now recognized that the a priori and the necessary don't always have to go together. One is an epistemological category, the other metaphysical, and they may not have the same extension. Kripke has suggested examples of necessary beliefs known a-posteriori and contingent truths knowable a priori (Kripke 1980). So it is not essential to the very idea of the a priori that necessity be tied to it.

Standard candidates for a priori knowledge are the truths of mathematics and logic. However, there are further truths that also seem to fit into the a priori, such as the belief that "something cannot be both red and green all over at the same time". Perhaps also such truths as "physical objects exist in space and time" and "time is infinite (or finite)" fit in. Logical beliefs do not have a specific content: they don't give any actual information about the world. For example "either *p* or not *p*" is true independent of what *p* is or whether *p* is true or false. There has been debate about whether mathematics is like this, or whether it does convey factual information. Yet there seems intuitively a difference between mathematics and logic and the other sentences mentioned above, called by Alberto Coffa "strange sentences" (Coffa 1976). These latter seem to convey important information about reality – truths of a very deep nature. They describe very fundamental features of reality, and so appear to have genuine factual content.

Epistemologists have tried to give an account of the kind of justification that could sustain all such truths, from those of logic to the "strange sentences". A classical account is the rationalist position, as expressed by Russell in *The Problems of Philosophy* and more recently powerfully defended by Laurence Bonjour in *In Defence of Pure Reason* (1998). This appeals to a notion of rational intuition. Such epistemologists typically begin by setting up a dichotomy: either we have a priori knowledge or we do not. They argue that the latter position leads to general scepticism and so should be rejected. Given, then, that we do have a priori knowledge, we need an appropriate explanation of how it works. Their general criticism of competitor theories is that they inevitably lead back to the sceptical dead-end of those denying the a priori. Against that, their explanation holds that humans have a certain kind of mental capacity allowing them to justify beliefs in a non-empirical manner. This is a part of our ability to reason in general. Much of our reasoning occurs inferentially: we move from premise to conclusion and see the connections between them. However, some instances of reasoning are non-inferential: we grasp truths immediately, without inferring them from other prior truths. So our grasp of such truths is direct, immediate and non-discursive. This grasp is not arbitrary or brute; it is, in fact, a paradigm of rationality. It is also irreducible: we cannot explain it in terms of anything more basic or fundamental. It in turn explains our inferential reasoning. For example, our understanding of basic inferential moves (e.g. *modus ponens* – from "p" and "p implies q" derive "q") is such that we grasp the general truth expressed in the paradigmatic example. This faculty supplies the principles fundamental to all our thinking: the laws of logic, the truths of mathematics and the other conceptual and metaphysical truths mentioned above.

What is the ontological status of these principles? What sort of things are they? The rationalist rejects the view that they are merely our ideas, that they have merely psychological reality. We form ideas of them, but they exist independently of our thought. Hence those defending this view generally tend to conceive of principles as abstract entities, having a non-empirical reality that is not merely mental. Traditional versions of this position have further held that such intuitions of these entities are infallible: they can't be mistaken, However Bonjour's more recent theory rejects this view, thus making it easier to defend. We have a fallible capacity to grasp truths of reason that exist independently of our thinking about them.

One of the main reasons why philosophers came to reject this account of the truths of reason is because of the emergence of alternative systems of a priori concepts, specifically the rise of non-Euclidean geometries. The axioms of Euclidean geometry are instances of principles purportedly known by rational intuition. The infamous fifth postulate of Euclid's system states, in effect, that given a point on a line there is no parallel to that line that also runs through that point. In the nineteenth century, various geometers explored systems in which this postulate was rejected. For example, the Russian Lobachevsky produced a system where many parallels were accepted; the system appeared coherent and seemed a viable formal system. A possible reaction to such a system was to dismiss it as a mere mathematical oddity, not having the application of Euclidean geometry, which is the true geometry of reality. Then, startlingly, Einstein argued that space is in fact curved and that non-Euclidean geometry is the correct system for expressing truths about real space. This provided a generally accepted scientific confirmation that what appeared to be the correct a priori system for understanding the nature of space was not in fact correct. How does this fit with the account of the a priori based on rational intuition?

If the rationalist account says that such intuitions are infallible, then the existence of non-Euclidean geometry is a clear counter-example to that position. However, if one defends fallible intuition the situation is less clear. One might say that geometers had a wrong intuition about Euclidean geometry, but that was corrected by a genuine insight into non-Euclidean geometry. However, the problem with this response is that Euclidean geometry isn't actually wrong or false, or whatever other normative term is appropriate. As a formal system it is consistent, which is the only appropriate test for such a system. We therefore have two systems of geometry (in fact, several systems). Each system is internally coherent. However, one system applies more readily to plane surfaces, and the other to curved surfaces. Space, considered in large cosmological terms, is best understood as curved. The terrestrial space of our immediate environment is largely conceived of as plane. Each geometry can describe both curved and plane surfaces, but Euclidean geometry is much simpler on plane surfaces and non-Euclidean geometry much simpler on curved surfaces. Rather than holding that there is the one true geometry of reality, one should hold that there are a variety of possible systems by which one can describe the reality of space. Pragmatic considerations such as ease of calculation and theoretical perspicuity will determine which one is selected in which context. Now, one might hold that this situation is still compatible with rational intuition of abstract principles. However, given the endless realm of such possible systems (limited only by mathematicians' imaginations) it seems that another account of our knowledge of such a priori systems is required, since we are now postulating a potentially infinite number of principles and acts of intuitive grasping of them.

The fact of a plurality of alternative geometries is an example of the existence of relative systems of a priori knowledge, chosen on pragmatic principles. But what of other such a priori systems, for example, simple arithmetic and basic logic? Are there any genuine alternatives to such systems?

On the rationalist account, there can only be one true a priori system in each field (e.g. one true geometry, one true maths, one true logic). The drive to this view comes from the belief that a priori intuition captures the one true deep nature of reality. If we have shown the possibility that there may be alternatives in some of the areas called a priori, then our general explanation of the a priori must be such that it can allow for alternative systems. This is not the same as saying there *must* be alternatives in each area. Rather the alternative to rationalism about a priori knowledge merely allows that in some areas (e.g. geometry) there may be alternatives, whereas in others (e.g. arithmetic) there aren't. A burden on this account is to provide a principled way of explaining why there are alternatives in one area and not another.

Now one such rival general account of the a priori is conventionalism, which was developed, among other reasons, to cope with the problems associated with alternative geometries. This holds that systems of a priori concepts, such as geometrical concepts, are conventions that are freely chosen, not forced on to us by the nature of reality. Systems of geometry may be used as different metrics – different ways of characterizing or cashing out what we mean by "space". We can supply varying ways of connecting up such metrics to observation: what are called "coordinative definitions". In developing a detailed scientific account of space we have an a priori element (the mathematical system of geometry), a bridging method (the coordinative definitions) and the rest of the scientific theory (views about the nature and speed of light, the properties of solids, etc.). One may change features in the metric (use alternative systems of geometry) that will have knock-on effects on the coordinative definitions and the scientific theory. This comes close to the holism espoused by Duhem, where any proposition may be preserved in a system as long as one is willing to make changes elsewhere. There are some problems about this in relation to geometry, which I'll discuss below, but let's initially move to somewhere where the problems seem more pressing, namely logic.

A conventionalist about logic holds that we establish the meanings of words in our language by conventions; we supply definitions of them. Certain words can be defined using the method of truth-tables elaborated by Wittgenstein in the *Tractatus*. These words are the logical constants "and", "or", "not" and "if . . . then". Logical propositions are those whose truth is only affected by these words, and not by any other words in the proposition. Thus "either p or not p" is true, irrespective of what p is. The definitions given in truth tables of "or" and "not" ensure that "either p or not p" is always true. Thus the logical truth "either p or not p" is a consequence of the definition of the terms that make it up. Conventionalism about logic holds that logical truths are consequences of linguistic definitions. These definitions are not constrained by the nature of any reality: abstract objects, the physical world or the nature of mind. They are free choices we make. Carnap expressed this view most forcefully, perhaps, in his *Logical Syntax of Language*, where he said:

> In logic there are no morals. Everyone is at liberty to build up his own logic, i.e. his own form of language, as he wishes. All that is required of him is that, if he wishes to discuss it, he must state his methods clearly, and give syntactical rules instead of philosophical arguments. (Carnap 1937: 52)

Carnap envisaged a multiplicity of such systems, analogous to the case in geometry. Ayer popularized this position in *Language, Truth and Logic* (1936), where the propositions of logic are analytical truths: truths by definition alone. They tell us nothing about the actual world, but are abbreviations of symbolism, true because of our linguistic conventions.

The advantages of such a position are immediately obvious. One doesn't have to postulate special mental faculties, such as intuition, to explain our grasp of the a priori. Such intuitions presumably are pre-linguistic and run the gamut of problems associated with privacy. Rather, our knowledge of the a priori is tied to our knowledge of language. Geometry is a system of definitions of terms, which can be connected by coordinative definitions to observation. Logic is likewise constituted by rules of language. We decide to accept certain moves in language and not accept others. It all happens in the open; there is no special ontology required and no special account of mind. Hence, it gives an account of this philosophically troublesome area of knowledge with little cost. Specifically, it gives an account of the a priori that meshes readily with empiricism, and empiricism had long been lacking an adequate account of the a priori.

Yet there are obvious objections to such a position. We aren't really free to make up logic as we like: it has an objective reality. For example, I just can't decide to allow an inference rule that produces contradictions. It would destroy the whole point of logic, which is to preserve truth in inferential moves. Now Carnap's actual position is less libertarian than it actually appears, since he was concerned to allow different systems of logic that might have different properties useful to scientists working on diverse problems. Hence, while he doesn't envisage any a priori constraints on the construction of logical systems, he does envisage practical constraints. We need to build systems that people find useful, and one that allowed wholesale contradiction would be spectacularly useless. There are other more technical problems with this conventionalism. What exactly is the status of the claim that all a priori propositions are analytical? If it is analytical itself, it just seems to be the consequence of arbitrary definitions and so has no compelling force. Why should anyone dubious of it accept it? If stronger than that it seems self-defeating – an instance of an a priori proposition that isn't arbitrary and analytical. Furthermore, consistency seems to be a required feature of all such systems. Is this a general necessary feature of all systems that must be explained in some way other than by claiming that it's an analytical truth? Finally, if we say that logical truths are consequences of the definitions of the logical constants, how, then, do we explain "consequence"? The notion of consequence is part of logic itself and so can't be presupposed in explaining the nature of logic. Quine makes this objection quite forcefully. Logic is so basic to our conceptual system, to our whole way of dealing with the world, that conventionalism relies on it, and not vice versa. To apply conventions in a systematic manner one needs to use a principle such as: "Whenever there is a case of type T we must apply convention C. This is a case of type T. Hence we shall apply C". If the convention in this case is *modus ponens*, the convention presupposes its own existence in order to be applied. Therefore linguistic conventions cannot be used to supply an appropriate epistemology for logic.

Rationalism had argued for an absolute conception of the a priori, which we have seen to be problematical. Conventionalism offered a solution that allowed for relativity about the a priori, but it is likewise beset with difficulties. Quine offered a more radical solution to the problem: he rejected the very idea of the a priori (see Quine 1976: 77–133). This is not to say that he denied that mathematics, logic or indeed many of the "strange sentences" exist and are useful to us. Rather, he challenged their epistemological status. Instead of conceiving of a sharp distinction between those propositions that are a posteriori, (and so keyed to experience), and those that are a priori (that are not so keyed), Quine boldly advocated a denial of the dichotomy and a reconstituted understanding of the issues in terms of a gradual spectrum. All beliefs are shot through with experiential input to some degree and all are theory laden to some degree also. None are wholly conceptual with no appeal to experience, and none are innocently just reporting brute experience. Some beliefs are really fundamental to the way we currently think about the world. The basic truths of logic and mathematics are like this, because if we were to alter them the repercussions would extend all the way through the rest of our beliefs. However, Quine also thinks that very general scientific truths, such as our views about gravity, relativity theory and so on are also deeply embedded like logic and mathematics. An alteration of them would also lead to wide-scale reassessment of our views about the world. Hence, he replaces the a priori–a posteriori distinction with a behaviourist account of our degree of willingness or unwillingness to abandon a belief in the face of recalcitrant experience. If an observation doesn't fit with our general theories, we can find reasons for discounting it as mistaken, or as some kind of glitch. If such recalcitrant observations persist, we have a choice about which things we would like to alter because of them. We could change physical theory, we could change logic or mathematics or we could change how we construe observation. There are various choices available to us.

There are certainly possibilities for relativism in Quine's general picture but, in so far as one is attempting to articulate an account of the a priori that is relativistic, a position that simply rejects the a priori won't work. The criticisms of Quine's position that seem most compelling are about meaning. The first is that Quine's views about the a priori are connected to his views about meaning and that these are unacceptable. He rejects the view that a theory of meaning (a theory of sense or intensions) is possible. All language must be viewed in an extensionalist manner. The arguments that lead him to deny that one can make the a priori–a posteriori distinction are those that lead him to deny a belief–meaning distinction. There is no principled way in which the distinction can be cashed out. The conventionalist view was that analytic sentences are purely linguistic, purely to do with meaning. Hence, considerations about language and meaning supply the epistemological basis for the a priori. In rejecting the analytic–synthetic distinction, Quine rejects the basis on which the conventionalists had drawn the a priori–a posteriori distinction. However rejecting the analytic–synthetic distinction also had the effect of rejecting the meaning–belief distinction. Some sort of meaning–belief distinction appears to be important for philosophy. We can consider concepts in themselves as distinct from concepts as used in sentences expressing truths about the world. Figuring out the meaning of the term "temperature" involves us in theory, in substantive beliefs about heat and its measurement. However, we can give an account of the meaning of the term and consider that independently from using it to express a belief. Quine had wanted to avoid the philosophical method that saw philosophers as analysers of meaning – sifting through an a priori realm of meanings and establishing the necessary connections between them. Philosophers should get their hands dirty and know substantive truths about the world, and not sit in armchairs and analyse meanings. The central point is that there isn't a realm of necessary a priori conceptual truths that are the province of the philosopher. One can accept this, but still hold to the view that issues about meaning are central to philosophy (even though meanings aren't separated from beliefs). One can consider meanings as temporarily fixed in order to see their implications, their conceptual role. Meanings do change and mutate, but the changed meaning has perhaps a new conceptual role, which it is likewise useful to clarify.

This is all the more important when considering the traditional provinces of a priori knowledge: mathematics and logic. One should think of these as pre-conditions for the articulation of a scientific theory, rather than elements of the theory itself. Even though there may be changes in these (for example, the changes in geometry discussed above), one can think of them as the mode of presentation – the form in which a theory is expressed. These can be examined for their properties, strengths, weaknesses and so on, and one can decide which one is better for particular purposes.

I shall call such a position on the a priori a pragmatist position. It differs from Quine in accepting that the a priori exists. It also differs in conceiving of the a priori as the realm of the linguistic pre-conditions for talk about the world and it differs in accepting that investigation of these pre-conditions is central to philosophy. In agreement with Quine it holds that none of these pre-conditions is absolute, and incapable of revision. Thus it rejects traditional meta-physical conceptions of necessity; necessity derives from the frame-work of concepts, and the patterns of those concepts are partly dependent on our choices. One can think of the a priori and the a posteriori in terms of a framework and that which is dealt with within the context of that framework. One is not committed to a single overarching framework for everything. There may be differ-ent frameworks (our geometry example). Indeed, what counts as content and what counts as framework may change over periods of time. What counts as a new bold discovery relative to one frame-work may be part of the accepted framework in a different setting. For example, at some stage it was a new discovery that gold dissolves in sulphuric acid. However, that quickly became a defin-ing feature of what counts as gold. In the first instance we had a new belief about what was antecedently picked out as gold. In the second case that belief has become an integral part of the meaning of the concept "gold". There is no hard and fast eternal distinction between what counts as belief and what counts as meaning; it is dependent on context and use. However, given a specific content and specific use it is very useful to distinguish between that which is accepted as pre-existing meaning and that which is accepted as a new belief.

This allows a fruitful way of thinking about the relationship between logic, mathematics and the "strange sentences" discussed above. They all belong to the meaning-framework – the realm of concepts by means of which we represent the world to ourselves and each other. Hence the proposition "physical objects exist in space and time" is a way of talking about what we mean by physical objects. It specifies the content of a concept that we have found extremely useful in characterizing our surroundings.

This pragmatist position can be found in a variety of writers who otherwise differ from each other greatly. It was adverted to in the section on frameworks in Chapter 1. C. I. Lewis presents it in *Mind and the World Order* (1956), describing philosophy as the investigation of the a priori, the a priori understood there as constituted by systems of concepts. Carnap has it in his distinction between linguistic frameworks and their contents (Carnap 1950). Wittgenstein proposes it in his distinction between the scaffolding of our thought and beliefs that presuppose that scaffolding (Wittgenstein 1969: §211). Lewis's linguistic Kantianism, Carnap's scientism and Wittgenstein's therapy differ greatly in how they think this insight should be used: for Lewis, it provides a way of continuing traditional philosophical reflection; for Carnap, it allows an eradication of traditional questions and a role for the philosopher as the analyst of meanings for scientists; and for Wittgenstein, it allows a gradual dissolution of traditional concerns.

The pragmatic position raises three important questions. First, how do we make sense of the notion of a framework itself? Is it explicit or implicit, natural or artificial? Secondly, is there a core framework that is, in fact, universal, or are there really a range of possible frameworks? Thirdly, how do we judge the acceptability, usefulness simplicity and so on of frameworks?

I think the best way of thinking about such a framework is that it is a tacit set of presuppositions operative in our general dealings with the world. A chief task of philosophy is to render explicit such presuppositions and to judge them. We judge them initially in an instrumental manner. What purpose do they serve and how well do they serve it? Philosophy also can attempt the deeper project of querying those purposes. Are there fundamental purposes (e.g. the pursuit of truth) or illegitimate purposes (e.g. the pursuit of selfish gain)? So while a framework is tacitly operational in all our talk about the world, it is made explicit by philosophical investigation. Unlike the case with Wittgenstein's philosophy, however, philosophy doesn't leave everything as it is. Philosophy actively tinkers with the framework, attempting to correct perceived problems and create new models – new ways of conceptualizing the world. In this it shares common cause with natural science; it just differs in scope and also asks more fundamental questions about the purpose of the concepts we use. In this way, we can begin to make more sense of the diversity of viewpoints that relativism seeks to defend. Viewpoints are keyed to purposes or ends. There may be more than one way to achieve a purpose and there may be a multiplicity of different purposes. The ontological relativity dealt with in Chapter 3 is a result of this diversity. One conceptualization of reality may be appropriate for some purposes (talking of particles and laws in order to gain mastery of the physical environment) and a different one for another purpose (talking of values and responsibility in order to build a just society). Which one is more fundamental? Well, that depends on which purpose is thought more fundamental and one might well think both equally indispensable.

But someone may still cavil and query whether there aren't basic universal a priori truths that hold no matter what framework is used, and whether these truths form the genuine realm of the a priori. While diversity may be possible in relation to what ontology we pick, and even in what geometry we use, there isn't really an alternative arithmetic or an alternative logic. So that brings us to our second question: is there a core framework?

In Chapter 2 I discussed the limitations on alternative logics and the centrality of the law of non-contradiction. In Chapter 5 I want to argue that the law of contradiction is one of the four principles of rationality that constitute a core conception of rationality. So I shall argue for a universal account of rationality. The third question is also answered by this core theory. How do we judge between frameworks? What sort of perspective must we take on them? In Chapter 5, an argument is advanced that we do, in fact, have a minimal theory of universal rationality that forms a universal framework – a universal precondition for all other frameworks. Built into this is an acceptance of non-contradiction. There will also be features of instrumental rationality that allow us to judge between frameworks and certain virtues of rationality that govern our reasoning. This universal core will provide sufficient critical leverage to allow reasoned disagreement – to provide the capacity to block an "anything goes" relativism – but still allows a great deal of legitimate diversity.

In conclusion, there is scope for relativism in epistemology. Contextualism and the pragmatic account of the a priori allow for differences in what counts as knowledge. However, by admitting this much relativism, one doesn't have to go as far as the extreme relativist position. Certain general features of rationality remain in place despite the contextual elements. Fleshing out what these features are is the topic of Chapter 5.

5 | Relativism about rationality

Core rationality

Advocates of relativism about rationality

Quite a number of writers have argued for alternative conceptions of rationality, but in many cases it is not clear what this means. A representative group of those views – taken from sociology of knowledge, anthropology, feminist theory and theology – will be discussed in this section. It will be argued that many of the "alternative" views presented can be accommodated within forms of relativism other than relativism about rationality – for example, as conceptual, ontological or epistemological relativism. Following this, a model for a non-relative account of rationality will be presented and defended. The subsequent three sections of the chapter will deal with the major lines of objection to such an account of rationality. The final section differentiates this approach from a famous attack on relativism by Donald Davidson.

Barry Barnes and David Bloor (see, for example, Barnes & Bloor 1982) have defended relativistic views about rationality, using themes from the sociology of knowledge. They reject universalist conceptions of rationality, holding that there are only local ones available, relative to context, culture, historical epoch and so on. They argue for this by insisting on the importance of investigating the empirical conditions under which beliefs arise for an agent, and showing how these are always local and particular. To counter the obvious objection that such a project merely focuses on causes rather than on reasons and so has nothing to say about rationality, they challenge the cause–reason distinction. They hold that supposed "evidencing reasons", which would hold universally, are illusory. They dismiss various standard candidates for such reasons. Appeal to sensory evidence manifests a naïve empiricism that falls to the challenge of the theory-laden nature of observation. Appeal to basic functional capacities, such as the ability to navigate the environment, are argued not to be basic at all, but rest on complex, culturally relative factors that have to be taught. The strategy that avoids this conclusion by claiming that such capacities are native, part of our biological inheritance, is shown to fall back to dealing with causes rather than reasons, and so goes back to the local empirical conditions under which belief is produced. They hold that there are no core beliefs or inferential practices for humankind that are paradigmatically rational. They appeal to the facts of cognitive diversity exposed by the sociology of science and to the failure of attempts by philosophers to establish foundations for such a core picture. They hold that deductive inference is actually unfounded or unjustified, since it could only be justified in a circular manner. To make such a justification, deductive inference would have to be used; hence there is no justification for deductive inference other than simply a blind faith in rationality. They wryly finish their case by noting,

> There is, of course, a final move that the rationalist can make. He can fall back into dogmatism, saying of some selected inference or conclusion or procedure: this just is what it is to be rational, or, this just *is* valid inference. It is at this point that the rationalist finally plucks victory out of defeat, for while the relativist can fight Reason, he is helpless against Faith. Just as Faith protects the Holy Trinity, or the Azande oracle, or the ancestral spirits of the Luba, so it can protect Reason.
>
> (Barnes & Bloor 1982: 46)

They then speculate on the causes behind such a massive profession of this faith by the philosophical community. Their position is clearly one advocating a vigorous form of relativism about rationality – it is local, contingent and empirically examinable.

Barnes and Bloor refer to some anthropological material in their work, but the American linguist Benjamin Lee Whorf (1897–1941) has probably made most famous the case from anthropological differences to alternative conceptions of rationality. He argues, drawing on an analysis of the language of the Hopi Indians, that languages contain different metaphysical schemas (Whorf 1956). There is no single universal set of categories that lies behind all language. Aristotle apparently believed that the subject–predicate structure of Greek reflected the substance–accident nature of reality, but Whorf's investigations revealed different linguistic structures to that of the Indo-European model and a different underlying metaphysics. He examined Hopi verbs, showing that while the language could pragmatically and operationally describe the observable phenomena of the universe, it rests on a set of abstract notions quite different from those of standard Western rationality. Western rationality is held to conceive of space as static, three-dimensional and infinite, while time is one-dimensional, uniform and ever-flowing. Whorf acknowledges that relativity theory conceives of space and time differently from this standard model but points out that the Hopi account is different again from either of them. There is a fundamental distinction in Hopi thought called the manifested–manifesting distinction, or as Whorf also describes it, the objective–subjective distinction. The manifested includes all that is evident to the senses, in the present and past (without distinguishing these). The manifesting includes all that is in the future, but also all that is mental (with a quite pan-psychist view of the mental) and, indeed, a quasi-religious sense of the awe-someness of the cosmos itself. Because this way of thinking about the world is so different from the standard Western scientific model, Whorf holds that he is only giving an approximation of it in his linguistic work – hence the two different characterizations of it. The importance of grasping the underlying metaphysics is that attempts to translate Hopi verbs fail without taking account of it: "without knowing the underlying Hopian metaphysics, it would be impossible to understand how the same suffix may denote starting and stopping" (Whorf 1956: 61).

Further examples can be adduced from other anthropological work, pointing to the empirical fact of cognitive diversity. There are varied beliefs about the physical world – for example, about forces and powers not recognized by Western rationality. There are beliefs about landscape of the kind described by Bruce Chatwin in *The*

Songlines, where Australian aboriginals believe that the landscape came into being through the agency of ancestor animals who sang the world into existence. Many cultures have other such cosmogonies. There are beliefs in Chinese culture about an energy or force that permeates all things – Chi – and which plays a central role in much traditional Chinese medicine such as acupuncture, or martial arts such as Tai Chi, or in philosophico-religious tracts such as the *Tao Te Ching* or the *I Ching*. Much discussion has centred on the views of the Azande, based on the work of the anthropologist E. E. Evans-Pritchard. The Azande believe that witchcraft is transmitted by unilinear descent from parent to child: a father's sons or a mother's daughters will be witches if the parent in question is a witch. They also believe that a post-mortem examination of intestines that reveals or fails to reveal witch substance is conclusive evidence indicating respectively whether one is a witch or not. These practices in themselves are quite divergent from Western thought. However, most importantly, if someone is examined after death and no witch substance is found, it doesn't clear the kin of suspicion. As Lawrence Simon says in a discussion of the issue, "The Azande may treat someone as a witch in spite of a clear deduction to the contrary conclusion from facts they accept. Yet the Azande do not seem to be aware of, much less concerned about, this apparent contradiction in their beliefs" (Simon 1990: 24). So they apparently accept contradiction – a major break from Western modes of thought.

Further challenges to the standard model of rationality come from feminism, which suggests that our ideas about rationality may be affected by gender issues and biased in important ways. Lorraine Code writes perceptively about feminist treatments of rationality and relativism (Code 1995). She notes the almost universal dismissal of relativism in late twentieth-century philosophy and points out that it generally has been a bad strategy for feminists to align themselves to relativism – that has had the tendency of further committing what they have to say to outer darkness. So many feminists are at pains to deny relativism. Nevertheless, she thinks it might be time for feminists to "come out" and declare for relativism. Their interest is in the contextualizing, historicizing and localizing of the epistemological project. Labelling this interest as "relativist" is an effective way of silencing it. However, Code challenges the very framework of the opposition between universalism and relativism. She claims it is part of a series of oppositions, such as reason–emotion, theory–practice, fact–value, mind–body and objective–subjective, which many theorists of all hues, not just feminist, have challenged. In opening up the terrain by showing a range of positions between universal and relative, a new style of project can be undertaken. Such a project is one in which it is possible to "reestablish a continuity between the rarefied concerns of the epistemologist and the messiness of everyday, practical knowledge seeking, where the commonsensical appeal of relativism attests to its pragmatic viability" (Code 1995: 19). The position that privileged a specific conception of rationality, as a universal abstract model, tended to "discredit women's knowledge, along with the knowledge of people judged to be unlettered and the knowledge produced by people of races, hues, and cultures different from those of the epistemology makers" (*ibid.*: 190). In such a way, the feminists' case can be seen to be similar to that of the non-Western case. However, Code doesn't hold with extreme relativism and believes that relativism is compatible with realism: that there is a real world to which we must answer. We do face irreducible facts in our experience and we don't invent the world at will. She thinks that part of the problem about our thinking about rationality is that we have been fed on what Wittgenstein had called a "one-sided diet" of philosophical examples – for example, simple perceptual examples or elementary propositions of physical science – which set the agenda of enquiry. Code suggests looking beyond these to wider questions about the social and political role of the knower, the honorific place of science and technology in industrial capitalist society, and the cultural results and implications of what we judge to be knowledge. She shows that feminists have brought to the foreground issues about the imperialism of claiming universal sameness – in ethnocentrism, androcentrism, classism and eurocentrism. Sensitivity to such matters is slowly beginning to permeate Western culture, reflected in legislation and social interaction. Furthermore, it is slowly beginning to affect epistemology, perhaps leading to a hesitation about simply writing-off eccentric views, such as that of the Azande (although, just as in the wider community, there are many epistemologists who would have no truck with such "politically correct" attitudes and who hold to what they see as the truth, *simpliciter*).

One can find another example of relativism about rationality in a traditional Western androcentric area of study: Christian theology. There is a school of philosophers, including Rush Rhees and D. Z. Phillips, associated with Swansea and following Wittgenstein, who defend what has become known as Wittgensteinian fideism. They hold that the rationality found in religious belief is *sui generis* and cannot be criticized from some external stance. Other recent philosophers of religion, influenced mainly by postmodernism, have argued for extreme cognitive diversity from what they regard as the collapse of modernist attempts to establish a universal account of human rationality. This is often called the collapse of foundationalism, although many different elements are conflated in this collapse (see O'Grady 2000). In the demise of this edifice, such philosophers advocate a religious worldview, not based on rational standards, but rather on aesthetic or other non-cognitive grounds. A fairly standard approach is to claim that there is a radical disruption in rationality; there are incommensurabilities between many different facets of contemporary culture and no single model of rationality to mediate between them. So, for example,

> it is at the most practical, the most "materialist" level that radical differences arise; in the same physical space one can build a cathedral or a nuclear power station, but there is no "commensurability" between the desire to build the one or the other, and the difference in the organisation of their structures, their configurations and symbolic evocations, is as great as that between the jargon of nuclear technology and the language of prayer . . ..Within our culture there are cathedrals and nuclear power stations, theologies and technologies, arts, sciences and so forth. In consequence, incommensurability is always already present. Besides endless overlaps, like the ground and the building materials common to both structures, there are also endless disjunctures, endless things not truly comparable, thought often in competition, because they have internal properties peculiar to their own size, position, speed, inclusion of other things . . .   (Milbank 1990: 343)

The point is that it is inappropriate to seek universal canons or standards of rationality with which one can indeed challenge any view expressed. As Barnes and Bloor argued, there is a reliance on faith, which is not answerable to any notion of rationality since rationality is regarded as just another competing faith.

All four areas discussed – sociology of knowledge, anthropology, feminism and theology – have postulated the need for alternative conceptions of rationality. However, it is not yet clear what is really involved in such a notion, since many of the issues and the examples cited can be explained by forms of relativism discussed earlier. Whorf's examples are clear cases of conceptual relativity, where different sets of categories are used and ultimately yield a different ontology. Code seems to be arguing for a widening of the scope and interests of the epistemologist, not necessarily to suggest a new model of rationality. The Zande and Chinese examples seem to involve substantive beliefs about reality. These might be regarded as false but, as discussed below, the mere falsity of a belief doesn't thereby make it irrational. Suppose, furthermore, that these beliefs are empirically adequate: they don't disagree with any empirical data available – they are sufficiently nuanced. Now, some have advocated rejecting unverifiable or unfalsifiable beliefs as meaningless. Yet this rejection has itself been devastatingly challenged as a form of untenable dogmatism. The vicissitudes of verificationism is a modern parable of the philosophical common sense of one generation being the object of ridicule of the next. If such alien beliefs could be construed as a form of trans-empirical metaphysics, then it is not at all clear that alternative conceptions of rationality are required in understanding and evaluating them. For example, Berkeley and Aristotle have very different metaphysical systems, but seem to share a great deal of assumptions about reason. So what is really involved in our notion of rationality and what does an alternative conception of rationality amount to?

A non-relativistic model of rationality

Rationality can be attributed to actions, emotions, beliefs and other attitudes. A rational action is one that is goal-directed by our reasoning: belief and desire combine to produce an action made appropriate by our reasoning. The most efficient action to bring about a desire, given one's beliefs, constitutes a rational action. At a basic level, one need not enquire into the truth or provenance of those beliefs. This kind of rationality is purely instrumental; *given* these beliefs and desires, this is the most appropriate response. For example, given John's belief that he is Napoleon, it is quite rational for him to seek to marshal his armies and buy presents for Josephine. Yet the belief that he is Napoleon requires evaluation. To evaluate such beliefs, one needs criteria of rationality. This is a stronger sense of rationality than the instrumental one relating to actions, keyed to the idea that there is quality control involved in holding beliefs. It is at this level that relativism about rationality arises acutely. Are there universal criteria that must be used by anyone wishing to evaluate their beliefs, or do they vary with culture and/or historical epoch? The burden of this chapter is to hold that there is a minimal set of such criteria.

Before attempting to defend a universal model for criteria of rationality, three preliminary issues need to be discussed. The first is that the view presented will be, following the standard epistemological usage, internalist rather than externalist. This places emphasis on the intuition that one may hold a false belief yet still be rational; rationality is not keyed to truth. Being reasonable means evaluating one's belief within a particular context. For example, ancient thinkers were mistaken in their views about the shape of the earth, but were not irrational to hold such views, given the information they had available. I may be mistaken in trusting my money to my bank manager, given that he's an incurable gambler teetering on the edge of a complete breakdown. However, since this was carefully concealed from me I was not irrational in giving my money to him. Yet doesn't this amount to relativism about rationality – making it context dependent?

The second distinction – a distinction between methodological and substantive conceptions of rationality – answers this in the negative. On a substantive view, certain beliefs are rational, and others are not, due to the content of the belief. This is evident in the common practice of describing rejected belief-systems as irrational – for example, the worldview of the Middle Ages is often caricatured in this way. Again, for example, believing in water spirits is irrational because there aren't any, while believing in traffic wardens is rational because, unfortunately, they are many of them. This substantive account is rejected because it boils down to the view that a rational belief is a true belief and an irrational belief an untrue one. A methodological view of rationality holds that it is not the content of the belief, but rather how one acquires the belief, how the belief fits with the rest of one's beliefs, and what one does with the belief, that determines its rationality or not. So there are no intrinsically rational or irrational beliefs (apart from contradictions): it is how beliefs are dealt with that is rational or irrational. Now, if one can identify a universal principled way of governing how to deal with beliefs, then one is not a relativist about rationality. Also, even given this methodological universalism, there can be a great deal of diversity in the details of the elaboration of one's set of beliefs.

The third distinction is between core and localized notions of rationality. Core notions are universal features in our treatment of beliefs. Localized notions are more specific features, which are not universal. For example, keeping the law of non-contradiction as a general overall principle is a universal feature of rationality, while discounting a particular person's testimony because I know them to be quite unreliable is a rational thing to do, but not universalizable. There are many such localized features of our rationality, relative to the context of discussion, the concepts used, the goals sought and the methodology used. For example, the means of seeking truth in law and physics differ. Seeking precedent is appropriate in one context of enquiry, and inappropriate in another. Statistical analyses are useful in psychological research, but perhaps not in aesthetics. Applying the standards of deductive logic in probabilistic contexts doesn't work. Aristotle noted this diversity when he said that,

> it is a mark of the trained mind never to expect more precision in the treatment of any subject than the nature of that subject permits; for demanding logical demonstrations from a teacher of rhetoric is clearly about as reasonable as accepting mere plausibility from a mathematician.
> (Aristotle *Nicomachean Ethics*: 1094b 24–7; 1976: 65)

But, given the diversity in forms of enquiry, methods, concepts and so on, there is not a total heterogeneity in forms of rationality. There are some features that cut across all areas – that hold good in all contexts. Gilbert Ryle caught this aspect of diversity and unity in rationality, nicely using the simile of travellers journeying:

> Different travellers use vehicles of highly intricate construc-
> tions and of very different makes for all the varying purposes of
> their very dissimilar journeys, and yet are alike in using the
> same public roads and the same signposts as one another.
>
> (Ryle 1954: 13)

The public roads and signposts constitute the core of rationality, used by all enquirers. So what is required is an account of these core principles of rationality that is internalist and methodological in the sense just described.

The model deals with two central components of rationality: logical coherence and evidence. It articulates four principles: a positive and negative requirement about each of these issues. The proposal is that these are broad enough to accommodate many of the insights about sensitivity to cultural, social and historical factors in our thought, yet have sufficient content to curb relativistic excesses tending towards scepticism or subjectivism.

Principle 1: Non-contradiction
Following the discussion of logic in Chapter 2, the first principle of rationality is non-contradiction. It will be accepted that the law of excluded middle is less central and may be dropped, as in intuition-ist logic. It is also possible that paraconsistent logics are acceptable in highly circumscribed contexts, but governed by criteria that accept non-contradiction. So there is a general presumption for all discourse that contradictions be avoided. We do, of course, make contradictions in practice, as fallible reasoners, but what is being established by this principle is a norm, a standard against which our practice is measured. Also, when we think it possible that a contra-diction is occurring, there are varying ways of showing how it doesn't have to happen. Sometimes the contradiction is only appar-ent and various other beliefs can be appealed to to show the lack of contradiction. Sometimes the concepts used are vague, or suffi-ciently nuanced to prevent a contradiction occurring. Some contra-dictions occur because of inattention; we don't realize that we contradict ourselves. What this principle holds is that we cannot be rational and consciously accept what we know to be a genuine contradiction.

Principle 2: Coherence among beliefs
Principle 2 derives from the principle 1 but is stronger. Principle 1 is primarily negative, in denying contradiction, but principle 2 seeks more positive links among beliefs. There are inferential connections between them – they constitute a logically coherent whole. There are evidential connections between them. Some beliefs stand as reasons for accepting others. This can include probabilistic relations, so the principle of coherence rules out probabilistic inconsistency – that we simultaneously hold "p" and "it is highly probably that not-p". This principle is an ideal; as limited thinkers with finite resources of attention and memory we will never achieve total coherence. However, striving to achieve coherence among our beliefs is a goal of rational methodology.

Principle 3: Non-avoidance of available evidence
We get evidence for our beliefs from many different sources: for example, perception, memory, inference and testimony. We use certain processes, such as inductive generalization from the past, as part of this whole process. We judge to the best of our ability on the basis of the evidence available to us whether a belief is true or false. We try to ensure that the evidence is reliable. This cuts across all areas of enquiry: the natural sciences, law, theology, history and figuring out who left the tap on that caused the bathroom to flood. This principle holds that we shouldn't avoid evidence available to us that will affect whether the belief is true or false. People of earlier times used all the evidence available to them to argue that the earth was flat. A modern person holding such a view would have to ignore the curvature of the earth observable through telescopes, satellite photography and the whole corpus of earth sciences and astrophysics, which deny the flatness of the earth. Such a modern person would be irrational because of the avoidance of available evidence.

Principle 4: Intellectual honesty
The fourth and final principle could be called the principle of intellectual honesty. Principle 1 was negative – avoid contradiction – and principle 2 a positive development of that – enhance coherence. Principle 3 was negative – avoid ignoring evidence – and now principle 4 is a positive development of that – maximize evidence. Why I called it the principle of intellectual honesty is that included

in it is the desire to find as much supporting evidence as one can for one's views, to evaluate competing views honestly and fairly, to assess counter-arguments and deal fairly with opposition. It calls for intellectual open-mindedness. It is what was lacking in Galileo's opponents, but also lacking in those who are dogmatic about whatever view and not open to the possibility that they could be mistaken – a vice not uncommon among philosophers and scientists.

These four principles together constitute an integrated core model of rationality. Principles 1 and 2 deal with coherence: the former a prohibition on incoherence, the latter advocating maximizing coherence. Principles 3 and 4 deal with evidence: the former a prohibition on ignoring available evidence, the latter advocating seeking all relevant evidence. The details of what might constitute relevant evidence and how coherence is to be tempered by the finitude of human cognition are left open, but the principles set the parameters of the discussion. Thus this model characterizes an approach to belief that is liberal in allowing a great deal of diversity in ways of construing ourselves and the world, yet strict in demanding certain conditions that those beliefs must meet in order to be called rational. How, then, does this core model deal with the examples of purported alternative rationality discussed above?

The Barnes and Bloor position holds that all evaluations and hence notions of rationality are local and non-universal. The stock response to that is to demand the status of that claim itself. Is it universal or local? Barnes and Bloor bite the bullet and hold that it is itself a local claim. Yet this stance is deeply problematical. It fails to engage with disagreement, since one who disagrees is, by the very fact of disagreement, in a different intellectual location. Precisely because it creates a situation where disagreement is impossible, it is an inadequate characterization of intellectual exchange. Barnes and Bloor themselves, on the view they espouse, couldn't hope to convince anyone other than those antecedently committed to identical views. The principle of non-contradiction is essential to the very possibility of debate and argument. While holding to a universal core theory of rationality one can also adopt contextualist notions of epistemology, entertain various logical systems and hold many categorizations of reality.

The anthropological examples can most readily be treated as alternative sets of categories. Are they rational? Well, as long as the account given as to why the Azande or Hopi hold to these categories obeys the four principles, they are. It could be argued that the Azande don't really accept contradictions. One can appeal to inattention (the Azande just don't bother about the apparent inconsistency, but don't endorse contradictions elsewhere), or perhaps to hidden beliefs resolving the contradiction (that when intestines are checked for witch substance by certain specific people – e.g. a chieftain – the kinship law doesn't operate, or that the purported parents weren't the real parents). Or perhaps their beliefs are nuanced in such a way that contradictions can't arise (witchcraft evidenced by kinship and witchcraft evidenced by post-mortem intestinal examination mean different things and so don't contradict). So there are ways of absolving the Azande from apparently accepting contradictions. In the case of the Hopi and the Chinese examples, it is clear that there is a coherent, developed worldview behind the categories used. The manifested–manifesting distinction and the concept of Chi both play important roles in an entire way of dealing with the world. Suppose the systems are empirically adequate – that they do not lead to empirical contradiction, they are coherent and the concepts in the system relate to each other in supportive ways. Do they fulfil the principle of not avoiding available evidence? In so far as they are empirically adequate, they do not contradict empirical evidence. However, they do cut against a materialistic or physicalistic metaphysics. There is therefore an argument possible between two competing metaphysical systems. Yet *qua* competing metaphysics, they are not irrational, although they may be false, underdeveloped or explanatorily deficient. However, a defender of such views – Chinese metaphysics, for example – can claim that his or her position purports to explain a broader range of phenomena than just physical change. It includes emotional, biological, moral, social and spiritual dimensions. In so far as one accepts these as important and non-reducible to the physical, one might rationally hold that Taoist metaphysics is superior to physicalist metaphysics, in that it explains a wider range of phenomena. This fits neatly with the point that arose in connection with Lorraine Code's feminist position. In expanding the range of topics that we regard worthy of intellectual investigation, we are not necessarily changing our conception of rationality, but changing the focus and use of our most useful intellectual tool: rationality.

With regards to the theological example, the model of rationality can show its teeth. The purported incommensurabilities appealed to, defending the fideist position, don't yield the result required. Differences between domains of enquiry are indeed evident, but that doesn't build up to the claim that each domain is sealed off from the others. The position articulated also seems contradictory, using what it purports to deny (universal canons of rationality). Its actual mode of argument is not of any local type or limited to a specific domain. It blithely deploys general criteria of rational acceptability to reject the notion of rational acceptability. It doesn't engage with relevant evidence, for there is much material on whether theism is defensible or not. Even if one comes to the conclusion that the debate is inconclusive, that very conclusion has to be reached using argument, and requires adducing evidence for the purported inconclusiveness and lack of evidence. So none of the purported examples of alternative rationality are convincing in dislodging the presumption of core rationality.

However, three initial objections may arise against this core model of rationality. First, it is purely formal, having little or no actual content, and so achieves very little against the relativist about rationality. Secondly, it places too great a stress on evidence to be a workable account of rationality. In certain contexts (e.g. being pursued by a bear) one doesn't wait to gauge competing evidential claims before acting and so this model doesn't apply to them. Thirdly, it is too ideal – it fails to connect with the actuality of human reasoning, which recent empirical research shows often falls below the ideal standards presented in this model. Hence the model is empty, not generally applicable and an unrealistic idealization.

The advocate of relativism about rationality holds that there are no universal features of rationality and no neutral stance from which to evaluate alternative frameworks. In so far as this core model holds against that view, it has content. It specifies four principles that allow evaluation and discussion across local differences. For example, there can be a rational discussion as to why certain kinds of reasoning are better for legal purposes and others for the purposes of physics. There can be rational discussion as to why checking chicken entrails for purposes of telling the future is not reliable. One can accuse someone of irrationality because of contravention of the principles; they are being inconsistent or ignoring some fact or other. Hence, although the principles are broad, they nevertheless do work. They allow for charges of irrationality to be made and provide a general framework of evaluation for enquiry in general. So, while quite formal, the model is not empty.

The principles are intended for the context of reflective deliberation. It would be crazy to deliberate when instant action is needed (e.g. avoiding the bear). One can indeed deliberate afterwards as to whether the instant action taken was the most appropriate, or at least adequate. So this model is intended not as a descriptive psychological account of what precedes any rational action, but rather is a normative model of the basic constituents of rational deliberation. It is generally applicable in all contexts of deliberation.

But human beings are not ideal cognizers: they have limited resources. So human beings cannot afford to be totally consistent in their beliefs. That is, they cannot spend a great deal of time scrutinizing their beliefs minutely for inconsistencies. Likewise, they cannot make all the inferential connections possible between their beliefs – since these are infinite – and hence cannot actually maxminize coherence among beliefs. So, too, with evidence: one can keep amassing evidence beyond the point of usefulness. The limits of our human situation place a curb on the extent or degree to which the principles are followed. This is the point made by Stich, detailed in Chapter 4. However such cognitive limitations do not mean that one has to abandon such a model. It serves as an aim or aspiration. Its purpose is normative – to guide cognitive activity. When trade-offs are made between, say, consistency and time available and importance of the beliefs in question, the very principles themselves are still operative in that process of making the trade-offs. When pragmatic decisions are made, instrumental rationality still operates, and obeys the basic model. Cognitive limitation is not a reason to deny a core model of rationality, or to suggest that massive diversity exists.

Despite all this, a friend of relativism about rationality might still be unimpressed. What has been shown is that some claims about alternative rationality can be accommodated within other kinds of relativism or contextualism. A core model of rationality has been articulated. Yet the relativist can claim that this is mere assertion; no compelling argument against relativism has yet been adduced. Specifically, important issues like the question-begging nature of the absolutist claim, and the problem of incommensurability have been neglected. The next few sections deal with these issues.

The causal challenge

I briefly presented the views of Barnes and Bloor in the previous section. I would like to work through the stages of their argument somewhat more systematically here. There are four main issues involved in their case. The first and most significant is a rebuttal of the claim that relativists about rationality refute themselves. The second is an attack on universal notions of evidence (denying principles 3 and 4 above). The third is an attack on universal conceptions of inference (denying principles 1 and 2 above). The fourth is a discussion of the argument about translating alien cultures. Since translation will be the focus of "The incommensurability challenge" (pp. 156–63), I shall defer discussion of it until then. Taking the other three points in order, I shall start with the question of whether relativists about rationality refute themselves.

I argued above that there is a *prima facie* case to be made that they do. In so far as relativists about rationality argue for their case, they presuppose universal conceptions of evidence and argument and so cut against the content of what they say – namely that there are not such universal conceptions. In so far as they do not argue for their case they can be ignored. However, relativists challenge this neat dilemma by pointing out that it assumes that which is at question. The argument only works if, indeed, there are universal rather than local conceptions of rationality. One cannot argue for universal conceptions of rationality by assuming as a premise that there are universal conceptions of rationality. The relativist holds that conceptions of rationality are local and so when arguing for his or her thesis, argues using local conceptions of rationality. Hence the universalist does not have leverage against the relativist in virtue of the fact that the relativist argues his or her case. The argument is conducted by means of local conceptions of rationality, issuing in a local conclusion, according to the relativist.

Now this certainly is a good response to the initial dilemma offered by the universalist and shows that a further case must be made for universalism about rationality. To do so one might question whether belief in universal standards of rationality operates as a premise in the argument, or as a precondition of the argument. If it is a premise, then there is problematical circularity. If it is a precondition, then circularity is not shown. How could it be shown to be a precondition? One line of argument ties rationality to the very idea of the content of assertion. In order to make an assertion at all, one has to obey certain conditions, which are universal and which operate as preconditions of discourse. For example, an assertion must possess a determinate content that holds universally. However, the relativist can again reply, why must they be universal, and why not merely local assertion conditions? The relativist maintains that the universalist again begs the question. Also, such a universalist position seems to make impossible an irrational assertion. If being an assertion is necessarily tied to strong conditions of rationality, then the very act of making an assertion guarantees rationality, which is too strong a result. Another line of argument is required.

A powerful intuition in favour of universalism about rationality is that localization renders intellectual disagreement difficult, if not impossible. Suppose Barnes and Bloor defend localized notions of rationality and I oppose them. By whose standards can this debate be resolved? On Barnes and Bloor's view there are no such standards. So on their position there is an intellectual impasse. Yet in defending localized views they make statements that seem at face value to be universalist.

> Numbers may favour the opposite position, but we shall show that the balance of argument favours the relativist theory of knowledge. Far from being a threat to the scientific understanding of forms of knowledge, relativism is required by it.
>
> (Barnes and Bloor 1982: 21)

> On the level of empirical investigation . . . there is more evidence to be cited for relativism than against it.   (*ibid.*: 24)

> The relativist, like everyone else, is under the necessity to sort out beliefs, accepting some and rejecting others.   (*ibid.*: 27)

By whose standards is this claim made? Does it merely apply in a local sense? What exactly is the explanation of the local context? Are there local contexts in which the four principles I articulated above don't apply? None of the anthropological evidence suggests that there are such locations. The general principles provide a framework within which a diversity of extended rationalities is possible. For example, I have not maintained that rational evidence is only scientific or empirical. A further issue is whether there are different modes of evidence possible in extended rationalities (for example, metaphysics doesn't rest on empirical evidence, but purports to explain it). I have, however, claimed that views based on different forms of evidence must cohere with each other. But that leaves a multitude of possible positions still open, without having to drop the requirement of a universal conception of rationality.

Barnes and Bloor defend themselves against charges of self-refutation by citing work by Mary Hesse, where she tackles the issue of the apparent self-refutation of their position (Hesse 1980). She reiterates the defence that, indeed, the standards they use are local standards. She amplifies this by saying that the relativists have redefined the terms "truth", "rationality", "cognitive grounds" and so on to "truth relative to the local culture", "rationality relative to the local culture" and so on. Cultures determine what these are. Presumably, when Barnes and Bloor speak of "balance of argument", "evidence" and "empirical investigation" these are to be interpreted as local notions. But local to whom? Do empirical investigations vary so that, in some other location, there is more empirical evidence against relativism than for it, as they claim? Does argument vary such that the balance of argument might be against relativism in another context? It seems clear that these terms are, in fact, intended in a universal sense. In her defence, Hesse goes on to unite relativism about truth with relativism about rationality, saying "[self-referential] consequences would only follow for those who retain a rationalist theory of knowledge, not for those who accept the redefinition of 'truth' and 'rationality' implied by their status as internal to given societies" (1980: 46). The kind of relativism about truth entailed by this notion of truth relative to culture was rejected in Chapter 2. The associated relativism about rationality is also to be rejected. The arguments presented by Barnes, Bloor and Hesse, if interpreted relativistically, have no strength against opponents of their views. If not interpreted relativistically, they are self-refuting.

Barnes and Bloor hold that all criteria of evidence are context-dependent. They make a distinction between absolute or context-independent judgements and local or context-dependent ones. The relativist denies the former and defends the latter. However, the absolute–local distinction is not the same as the context-independent–context-dependent distinction. One can make a judgement that is highly contextualized, yet nevertheless holds true in an absolute way. Statements involving indexicals (i.e. with references to specific times and places) are good examples. When I utter of myself at time t and place p that "I am at t at p", then it is absolutely true. It would be false if any one of the highly contextual factors were not in place; nevertheless it is as true as any sentence is likely to be. Given a framework of assumptions, there is an absoluteness about the judgement, relative to those assumptions. Now relativists about rationality typically ignore this kind of absoluteness and instead point to the contingency as they see it of the set of assumptions. However, such relative absoluteness (if I might put it thus) is an important feature of belief and is not itself relative to anything further.

Why this is important to note is that the relativist's strategy is typically to show that when a belief is relative to a set of background beliefs, that background set is itself not necessary, or fixed or infallible. For example, "something is only evidence for something else when set in the context of assumptions which give it meaning" (Barnes & Bloor 1982: 29). However, non-relativists about rationality don't need a foundationalist grounding for the background set. They focus on the relationship between the foreground and background beliefs. The principles of rationality expressed above are all methodological features of the relationship between foreground and background, which yield absolute judgements of rationality despite the contingent or fallible nature of both. For example, the metre is an arbitrary unit of measurement. It could have been longer or shorter. It has a history of being decided on, having a paradigm set up and a social history of its use (or pointed non-use by partisans of imperial measure). Nevertheless, when I say "the distance between home and work is 8 km", I make an absolute judgement. It is dependent on the contingent context, but given that background it holds true. I could say "the distance between home and work is 5 miles", but that is an instance of conceptual relativity. Given a different set of concepts, of background assumptions, I can still make an absolute judgement.

Barnes and Bloor argue against universal criteria governing evidence by repeatedly showing that such criteria will always include contextual elements and are fallible. They hold that appeal to experience ends up in a form of naïve empiricism, or that appeal to certain native biological skills also involves social factors and, anyway, these skills count more as causes than reasons. These points may hold good against traditional forms of foundationalist empiricism, which seek an infallible foundation in experience for our knowledge. However, they do not hold against fallible naturalistic epistemologies. Such approaches can show how causes can be reasons, when the cause of a belief is statistically likely to produce a true belief in specified conditions (e.g. an empirical account of perceptual belief-formation). To get rid of the requirement for infallible reasons is not to get rid of the requirement for reasons, even if fallible and contextually nuanced.

They also argued against universal views about inference. However, their arguments are for scepticism about logic rather than relativism about logic. They hold that no justification of deduction can proceed without using deductive processes. Hence, no noncircular justification of deduction is possible. Therefore, no justification of logic is possible (leaving aside for now the irony of arguing for this). The implication of this is no logic at all, and not multiple systems of logic, as they take it. As with their discussion of empirical evidence, the point is well taken against an opponent who wishes to defend strong theses about the nature of logic and its foundations. Such views of logic typically tied it to the nature of being or the nature of mind – having a heavyweight metaphysical underpinning to it. Similarly, views of logic that made it analytic in a strong sense of that term, constituted by the meaning of the logical connectives, fall prey to a variety of powerful arguments (many deployed by Quine). Nevertheless, a naturalized, post-Quinean view of logic can accommodate the qualms of Barnes and Bloor. Logic is an integral part of our web of belief. It isn't justified separately from the rest of our beliefs – there isn't a foundation on which it all rests. Yet without it we just don't make sense. Certain aberrations from standard logic are possible, but there is a universal norm based on non-contradiction. To hold that logic isn't justified in some special way distinct from other kinds of beliefs is not to hold that logic is merely held on faith, or is "irrationally" held. Again, there is confusion between infallible and fallible reasons. When one rejects infallibility, one doesn't *ipso facto* reject rationality.

Let us turn now to another issue pressed by relativists, the question of incommensurability.

The cultural challenge

Philosophers have used information gleaned from cultural anthropology to challenge the idea that there are universal standards of rationality. The claim is that what is being presented as universal is, in fact, culturally relative. The notions of rationality prevalent in post-Enlightenment, Western, liberal democracies are different to those of other cultures. So examples are brought forward from different cultures to argue that very different criteria of rationality are in operation in them. One particular example that has been widely used in philosophical discussions is that of the Zande tribe.

The British anthropologist E. E. Evans-Pritchard lived among the Azande (Zande singular and adjectival) in the late 1920s and published his account of an important aspect of their culture in *Witchcraft, Oracles and Magic among the Azande* in 1937. The tribe lived in the southern part of the Anglo-Egyptian Sudan, and had been studied independently by French Dominican missionaries and a British colonial official. Evans-Pritchard noted how their ideas of magic and witchcraft were deeply intertwined with their everyday practices, being an inseparable part of their culture. They believed that ill-fortune was the result of the activities of witches and sorcerers. They consulted witchdoctors to counteract the magic of the witches and they used different kinds of oracle to divine the truth about the activities of witches. So the Azande believed in an elaborate system of occult powers, psychic agents and divination processes that had no basis in a scientific view of reality. Furthermore, they apparently accepted contradictions among their beliefs. They believed that witchcraft was transmitted from father to son and mother to daughter and that the kin of a witch are also witches. However, in practice they only treat close paternal kinsmen of a known witch as witches. So their beliefs about the identity of witches contradict themselves, but they accept both sides of the contradiction. Hence the Azande believe in an elaborate reality that most Westerners would reject, and also seem to embrace contradictions. The philosophical claim is that they stand as examples of people who have a different kind of rationality. Their beliefs are complex and largely systematic and should be accepted as an alternative kind of rationality.

However, many think this is too quick a conclusion. Various others would be tempted to write off the beliefs of the Azande as primitive and/or irrational. In fact, in theoretical accounts of such belief systems, one can identify at least five stances in interpretation, only one of which is the relativist position, defending alternative conceptions of rationality: intellectualist, mysterious, pre-logical, symbolic and relativist.

The first can be styled the "intellectualist" position. This holds that the Azande are rational, but mistaken in their beliefs. They use evidence in recognizable ways and generally accept deduction and induction, but end up with beliefs that do not match reality – perhaps being akin to medieval Europeans. The "mystery" position says that we are condemned not to understand such tribes at all; we have no genuine access to their belief systems. Our Western belief system is at such a far remove from theirs that no genuine contact is possible. The "pre-logical" position holds that such tribes use a kind of pre-logical or mythic thought that differs from rational thought. So, while not an alternative kind of rationality, it is a different kind of thought. The "symbolic" position holds that the beliefs are not literal, but rather are symbolic and expressive, being an expressive reaction to the vicissitudes of fate and also a force for social cohesion. The final stance is the "relativist" position, which holds that the Azande have a genuinely alternative system of rationality, which cannot be judged by the standards of a different system, such as the Western scientific system of rationality, and it is this latter which is most of interest here. However, some comments can be made on some of the other stances first. The mystery position seems too strong. It would seem to render impossible the empirical study actually achieved by Evans-Pritchard, who presented such exhaustive detail on the Azande. The pre-logical position was, in fact, withdrawn by its proponent (Levy-Bruhl) in his later writings.

It differs from the relativist about rationality in suggesting a non-rational alternative to Western rationality. For argumentative purposes, however, it can be assimilated here to the relativist position, holding that there are alternatives to a universal account of rationality, and will be discussed as such below. The symbolic position is problematical because it seems to remove or render unimportant the actual reasons put forward by the Azande for their beliefs. The Azande really believe in the power of witches and the efficacy of witchcraft against that power. The symbolic interpretation says that these reasons are unimportant and that what really is going on is an expressive way of dealing with uncontrollable forces in the environment, like disease and death. As an interpretation it cannot explain the intentions of the natives, but operates only at a remove. It might be workable as a causal account of the origins of some of the beliefs, but doesn't explain the beliefs from the agent's point of view. So the two main contending positions left are the intellectualist versus the relativist position. The position on universal principles of rationality defended in the first section of this chapter is intellectualist. So what sort of arguments can a relativist bring forward to advance their position?

Probably the most famous such argument comes from the work of Peter Winch, who draws heavily on the later work of Wittgenstein. He articulates the relativist position in two main works: the book *The Idea of a Social Science* (1958), and the 1964 paper "Understanding a Primitive Society" (1970). In the book he argues that social sciences have a different methodology from that of the natural sciences. When investigating social events one has to understand not merely causes, but motives. Winch claims that such an investigation is not possible just using the kinds of concepts used in natural science, but following Ryle says, "to speak of a person's motives is not to speak of any events at all, either mental or physical, but is to refer to his general dispositions to act in the ways in question" (Winch 1958: 80). Winch adds to this that understanding motives means understanding the standards governing life in the society in question. Particularly in relation to the arts and religion, the interpreter of such phenomena must share sensibilities with the people deploying the terms, which is different from the procedure of a natural scientist.

Winch draws on Wittgenstein's use of the terms "language game" and "form of life". Language games are constituted by rules of grammar, which legislate for the use of concepts within them. Each language game has its own rules. Language games are associated with forms of life, which are the kinds of activities out of which the use of language emerges. In Wittgenstein's own usage, language games are quite specific uses of language, such as playing a game, or builders moving slabs, or buying an apple. He deploys them to attack a certain conception of how language works. However, with Winch, the scope of Wittgenstein's thought is broadened. Societies can have their own distinctive linguistic and conceptual uses, or religion and science can have distinctive "language games". He explicitly denies that there are overarching criteria that cross all domains. Hence "criteria of logic are not a direct gift of God, but arise out of, and are only intelligible in the context of, ways of living or modes of social life" (Winch 1958: 100). Concepts and ideas only gain sense in a context and the notion of "reality" only gains sense in a context. "The check of the independently real is not peculiar to science" (Winch 1970: 81). "Reality is not what gives language sense. What is real and what is unreal shows itself *in* the sense that language has" (*ibid*.: 82). Specifically in relation to the Azande, Winch rejects the view that says that European modes of thought are right and the Azande are wrong, for "standards of rationality in different societies do not always coincide" (*ibid*.: 97). Winch's more positive interpretation of the Azande has to do with relating their magical rites to a sense of the significance of human life. We can learn from such people new possibilities about human existence; in this context he cites Simone Weil's critique of the means of production in Western technological society. The standards we Westerners uncritically accept may be flawed and unacceptable. They lose out on certain things that perhaps the Azande appreciate. In similar vein, Robin Horton finishes his comparison of African thought and Western science by noting that he chooses to live in Africa, because

> one certain reason is the discovery of things lost at home. An intensely poetic quality in everyday life and thought, and a vivid enjoyment of the passing moment – both driven out of sophisticated Western life by the quest for purity of motive and the faith in progress. How necessary they are for the advance of science; but what a disaster they are when they run wild beyond their appropriate bounds. (Horton 1970: 170)

However, Horton does not find it necessary to postulate alternative modes of rationality to articulate these views. While Winch has rightly drawn important distinctions between the natural and social sciences, emphasized the need for sensitivity in understanding different cultures and warned about complacently accepting the prejudices of our own culture, he doesn't have to defend these by appeal to alternative systems of rationality. Indeed, there are important arguments that can be deployed against using the notion of alternative systems of rationality in the cultural context.

There are, firstly, some empirical points to note. Anthropologists, out of professional interest, tend to focus on the alien or strange aspects of a culture and devote time and attention to these. The mundane, familiar modes of thought are not of interest to them, but should be to philosophers who want to argue for alternative rationalities, since a great many basic transactions in such cultures are continuous with people everywhere. Evans-Pritchard says of the Azande, "Most of their talk is common-sense talk, and their references to witchcraft, whilst frequent enough, bear no comparison in volume to their talk about other matters" (1937: 20). Furthermore, if cultures have their own standards of rationality, one would expect them to be immune to intellectual challenge from without. But in the history of traditional cultures, one can see a pattern of old beliefs dying out in the face of new systems (the prevalence of ghost stories in rural Ireland waned in the aftermath of rural electrification). This shouldn't happen if there are genuinely alternative rationalities.

There are also important philosophical points against the possibility of such alternative rationalities. In order to understand a traditional society such as the Azande, one has to translate their language into one familiar to the anthropologist. The process of translation itself has a number of presuppositions. All one has available are the verbal utterances of the native and the translator's perception of the situation while translating. The translator has to ascertain the utterances that signify assent and dissent. In so doing, the translator projects a system of logic, with notions of contradiction, identity and inference, on to the native, since that is the translator's understanding of the yes–no idiom. Furthermore, the translator has to assume that the native is seeing more or less what the translator sees and his or her statements are connected to the

things in the environment. These are presuppositions of the translation process. They can be subsequently fine tuned, but are required
for the very possibility of translation. To understand the native
language, one has to presuppose that they share a great deal of our
way of thinking about the world. This cuts against the claim that
there are radically divergent rationalities.

Finally, Winch has correctly argued that understanding meaning
is context specific. To grasp the correct application of a term, one has
to see its relationship to connecting terms in a system of interrelationships. However, given that understanding meaning is context specific
in this way doesn't entail that truth-claims using such meaning-
systems have to be evaluated in different ways. Given that words used
in science and in religion require importantly different understandings, it doesn't follow that truth claims made in each domain
have to be evaluated using different modes of rationality. If someone
argues in religion for a fourth member of the Christian Trinity, or for
the importance of the fifth evangelist, the arguments rebutting him
or her will crucially involve notions like coherence, evidence, testimony and accuracy – notions at work in all other intellectual areas.

It is true that Western interactions with traditional cultures have
generally been to the disadvantage of those cultures. It is also true
that anthropologists in the past have been guilty of cultural prejudices about the objects of their study, assuming, uncritically, their
own superiority and that of their culture. However, a swing to the
opposite pole of denying any possibility of critical evaluation of
such cultures is too extreme (I am not claiming here that Winch's
actual position involves such a strong claim – although it could be
pushed in that direction). It is important to be able to make a call on
the relative truth-claims of such cultures. The task of a core model
of rationality is to allow for such critical engagement without
necessarily pre-judging the issue on one side or the other. But the
important point here is that the data from alien cultures and the
philosophical arguments about them are not at all compelling on
the possibility of alternative systems of rationality.

The incommensurability challenge

Some ideas of Thomas Kuhn, pertaining to relativism, were introduced in Chapter 1. In the arguments for relativized accounts of

rationality, his idea of incommensurability looms large, a major weapon in the relativists' arsenal. While the way Kuhn expressed his thought in *The Structure of Scientific Revolutions* (1970) lent itself to a strongly relativistic reading, Kuhn himself has been at pains to temper that interpretation in subsequent work (e.g. Kuhn 1977, 1993). Since a key relativist claim is that there are different paradigms of rationality, the notion of paradigm itself needs to be examined, and how it leads to claims about incommensurability needs clarification. But first, incommensurability itself needs clarification, since a number of different claims are typically associated with the term.

The term "incommensurability" derives from mathematics and arose in discussions of Pythagoras's theorem. That theorem says that in a right-angled triangle, the square of the hypotenuse is equal to the sum of the squares of the other two sides. This is easily demonstrated when, for example, the lengths of the sides are 3 cm, 4 cm and 5 cm. Then the measurement is possible in whole numbers: $9 + 16 = 25$. Such sides are "commensurable": they can be measured using common units. However, if one was to move to other numbers, such commensurability breaks down. The length of the hypotenuse of a triangle with sides of length 6 cm and 7 cm will not be a whole number. It is "incommensurable" with the others.

As Kuhn uses the term, it means that paradigms don't neatly fit with each other: there isn't ready comparison of one with another. This has philosophical implications in two areas. First, it has implications for meaning. If two languages are incommensurable it means that one cannot translate between them. Since they are isolated from each other the terms and idioms of one just do not find a correlate in the other language. It could be that whole worldviews are incommensurable in this way. For example, one could claim that the worldview of the Azande is incommensurable with that of the typical modern Western scientist – they just don't understand each other. Secondly, incommensurability has implications for evaluation. If two domains of discourse are incommensurable, one cannot be judged with the standards of the other. There is no platform outside those domains that provides a neutral vantage point. These two doctrines – meaning incommensurability (MI) and knowledge incommensurability (KI) – are logically different claims. MI entails KI, but the reverse entailment doesn't necessarily hold. If two realms cannot afford grounds for mutual understanding in terms of meaning, then knowledge judgements cannot be made either; therefore MI entails KI. However, it is possible to conceive of one understanding the meaning of a realm, but holding that one cannot judge as to the truth or rationality of the claims made in it. Hence KI doesn't entail MI.

Furthermore, there are variations in the strength of claim that can be made for incommensurability. Global incommensurability holds that all parts of a language or worldview are incommensurable; local incommensurability holds that only certain parts are. Different possible positions concerning incommensurability are therefore global MI, global KI, local MI and local KI. How do Kuhn's thoughts about paradigms and scientific revolutions bear on these positions?

A key thought in Kuhn's work is that scientific observation is not a neutral bedrock on which theory rests, but is radically affected by theory. He rejects the "development by accumulation" model of science implicit in the view that observation is neutral – that there are fixed methods that produce knowledge by accumulating more and more facts. To the contrary, when scientists are being trained, they are inducted into a practice, a set of assumptions, puzzles, methods, applications of theory, use of instruments and so on. This gives them a way of looking at the world and a range of problems on which they can work. This whole complex *modus operandi* is what constitutes a paradigm. It functions as a matrix for the production of scientific knowledge and has had clear success in dealing with particular problems. It is broader than merely a set of rules or procedures, and so is closer to the idea of a worldview. Kuhn's method is avowedly historical and developmental, looking at key periods in the history of science and thereby gaining an understanding of progress in science. This contrasts with the largely static model of understanding science that preceded him. By examining, for example, the Copernican revolution, the discovery of oxygen, the development of the theory of electricity or the Einsteinian revolution in physics, he portrayed the process of scientific development. It follows the pattern of initially having "normal science": a stable paradigm that functions as the matrix described above. Then various anomalies appear that cannot be resolved in the paradigm. As these become more pressing, a period of crisis emerges. A new matrix begins to develop. It is difficult to tell whether it will be a genuine advance or not. Scientists are pulled one way and another; insecurity and resistance to change are much in evidence. Yet eventually a new theory, with new assumptions, applications, problems and its own internal puzzles, wins the day. Adherents to the old view are sidelined and the new paradigm attracts the best contemporary talent.

Kuhn describes such a change in paradigm as a revolution. Like political revolutions, a certain element of anarchy is present. There is no higher standard for paradigms than acceptance by the community of scientists. He likens paradigm change to a *Gestalt* switch (except that it is usually irreversible). Implications of subjectivism arise at this point. If acceptance by a community of scientists is indeed the only criterion of evaluation, it makes the validity of science dependent on what a group of people think at a particular time (and suppose they are all drugged by a dictator and do "Nazi-science"). Typically, one wants to think that they could be wrong and there are standards beyond mere group acceptance. Also, describing the shift as a *Gestalt* switch implies that it is in some sense non-rational – it just happens, it isn't the end of a reasoning process. These features of Kuhn's work (which he subsequently strove to temper) gave impetus to arguments for relativism about rationality. If "paradigms" encompass all that counts as being rational in a given situation, and if there are different paradigms with no overriding system of adjudication, then this seems to establish global KI or, in other words, relativism about rationality.

Furthermore, as I said above, MI implies KI. Kuhn seems to defend the former and in so doing commits himself to the latter. The meaning of key terms in a paradigm derives from their place in the network of concepts and assumptions of the paradigm. Removed from that context they have a different meaning. The use of a term in one paradigm is different from its use in another and so the meaning changes. Hence the use of the notion of paradigm provides reasons for espousing MI and therefore KI. Now, are these to be understood in global or local terms? Kuhn makes some statements that indicate that they are to be understood globally, for example speaking of scientists before and after a revolution as "working in a different world" (Kuhn 1970: 118, 135). However, he also says things that could lead to a local construal: for example, "the world of his research will seem, here and there, incommensurable with the one he inhabited before" (*ibid.*: 111).

As might be recalled from the start of this chapter, proponents of alternative rationalities appealed to incommensurability to defend their position and they understood it in a global sense. Furthermore, they defended both global MI and global KI. In the context of Kuhn's own work, these strong theses will not hold because they undermine the very project he has attempted to undertake. If the claim is that terms cannot be understood outside of the paradigm in which they are used, then one cannot compare paradigms in the way Kuhn has done. For example, the story of the competing views of Lavoisier and Priestly couldn't be described in the aftermath of Lavoisier's triumph, if global MI were true. Furthermore, it would be impossible to tell if theories were genuine rivals or not if the thesis held. To establish rivalry some common ground is required. If claims of global KI were true, then it would be impossible to tell whether a new paradigm was more successful than another at answering anomalies for the old paradigm.

Proponents of alternative rationalities may be prepared here to claim that science in its totality constitutes a paradigm in their sense, but there are other such paradigms – for example, non-Western cultures, women's rationality, religion, magic and so on. It would make sense that Kuhn's examples aren't, in fact, incommensurable, since they all belong to the same large-scale paradigm: Western science. However, this is incommensurable with these other paradigms. Can this claim stand?

To oppose this claim, and try to defend a universal model of rationality, it is useful to look at some of the assumptions in Kuhn's account of paradigms. Standard philosophical lore has it that Kuhn and Quine inaugurated the demise of logical positivism in the late 1950s. However, recent historical work has shown how variegated and nuanced the logical positivist's position was, espousing holism and the theory-laden nature of observation, articulating anti-private-language arguments and supporting various forms of relativism (see, for example, Friedmann 1999). As part of that process, key features of positivist thought can be seen to continue in both Quine and Kuhn. All these thinkers were non-cognitivists about ethics. This further manifested itself in distrust of rules and normativity. For the positivists, these were "conventions", pragmatically useful but with no significant theoretical role. Carnap's discussion of linguistic frameworks prefigured Kuhn's discussion of paradigms. There was no principled way of distinguishing between frameworks; it was a matter of convenience. Likewise, Kuhn's account of paradigms holds that there is no framework within which one can adjudicate alternative frameworks – it is a matter of contingency, historical accident. However, the core rationality model presented above does give a framework that can be used, centrally appealing to consistency, coherence, non-avoidance of evidence and seeking relevant evidence. The paradigm changes within science are governed by these considerations. So, also, different modes of thinking, such as non-Western cultures, theology, feminism and so on, can be seen to hold to these minimal standards too. Global KI is a doctrine that fails to find coherent articulation, since any attempt to articulate or defend it will subscribe to these minimal standards.

Could there, nevertheless, be a case for local incommensurabilities – that in some areas there are ideas or cognitive practices which just can't be compared with others from without? This local incommensurability is a common enough feature in cultures where things are held to be so dissimilar as to be incomparable – the phenomenon of "chalk and cheese". We often accept that tastes are incommensurable; we can't compare likes and dislikes, say, my liking for olives compared with your dislike of them. At a less trivial level, do we think that a career as a teacher is better or worse than that of an opera singer? It is hard to say. We might be inclined to say it is undecidable (all other things being equal with regards to personal leanings, salary, career opportunities and so on). These local incommensurabilities don't add up to anything very significant about alternative rationalities. To be significant an incommensurability would have to be global.

However, one might suggest that certain cultures do have incommensurable attitudes to the world that result in very different conceptions of the world. For example, David Wong (Wong 1989) has suggested the difference in attitude to the world of traditional Chinese society compared to the attitude of Western science. For the former, a notion of "attunement" to reality is very important. The advances of science are not to be welcomed at any cost. The difference rests in the primary values of the people involved. In Western society there is a general acceptance of scientific developments, but also growing alienation from technological society. In traditional Chinese thought, the impact of any such scientific development on "the good life" was of primary importance, trumping any instrumental value gained by technology. We could perhaps call this value incommensurability (VI) and contrast it with MI and KI, discussed above. While sympathetic to this view, I do not believe it implies any doctrine of alternative rationality. There may be different values espoused, different conceptualizations of reality, alternative ontologies involved, but all this diversity is compatible with a universal standard of what counts as core rationality.

A significant rejection of this universalism about rationality can be found in Alasdair MacIntyre's work. He holds to the view that there are incommensurable traditions of thought that embody their own criteria of rationality and that deny a neutral high ground from which to evaluate them in a neutral fashion (for example, MacIntyre 1989). A quick response is to wonder which tradition MacIntyre inhabits and how he manages to discuss and evaluate the ideas of so many people from other, apparently incommensurable, traditions. A longer response is to accept that there are enormous differences between cultures and historical periods, but to challenge the view that these differences are best characterized in terms of differences in rationality. MacIntyre uses a wealth of historical material to make his points. He discusses many cases where two incommensurable cultures come into conflict, and chides defenders of universal conceptions of rationality for having "a certain lack of sociological imagination" (MacIntyre 1989: 184). One of his examples (close to his heart) is that of the differences between Irish Gaelic speakers and English settlers of 1700, which I'll focus on as a speaker of both languages. His claim is that there are two sets of languages that are incommensurable, embodying different value systems, systems of evaluation, systems of social relationships and so on. It is quite true that there are differences between these groups, and the central point of concern is how exactly to characterize the differences. Take a modern, less politically fraught, example of difference. In the day-to-day running of my philosophy department we differ from our neighbouring university. We use different terms (second years are senior freshmen), different methods of organization (a four-year instead of a three-year degree) and different decision procedures (the staff member in charge of a year can decide whether to accept late student essays at his or her discretion, instead of the head of department deciding). So we have differences in vocabulary, social structures and justification procedures. But, crucially, no one would claim that these differences amount to a different system of rationality. They are differences that can be argued for and justified internal to an overarching system of rationality. Now let's go back to MacIntyre's example of eighteenth-century Ireland. The native population had a distinctive religious system, bardic system and agricultural system, which came into conflict with a new culture (of course the "native" system was a mix of many different elements – Celtic, Norse, Norman, Elizabethan English, Spanish, Italian – are these all commensurable?). The Irish and English systems differed dramatically and the clash wasn't mediated by rational exchange but by force, coercion and all the usual trappings of cultural takeover. Yet nothing in all this postulates the need for a view that they differed in rationality – that the Irish reasoned differently to the English. Indeed, one of the main propagandist planks of cultural clashes such as this is to claim that such differences do exist, that one culture is dramatically inferior to the other with regards to rationality, as the propagandist cartoons such as those of *Punch* illustrated. Differences can be articulated as having different vocabularies, different systems of concepts and different systems of justification, but there are also underlying common features beneath the differences. Argumentation *qua* argumentation follows the general principles articulated in "Core rationality" (pp. 131–46), and the Irish of MacIntyre's example had elaborate systems of argument that obeyed the universal principles of rationality.

But in that case is there any incommensurability left at all, or is everything luminously clear, as the Enlightenment would have wished? To further discuss this I shall turn to the arguments of Donald Davidson. I shall criticize his strong rebuttal of incommensurability and in so doing we'll reach some conclusions about what's left of the idea.

Davidson's argument

Donald Davidson (1917–) has developed a formidable philosophical system, expressed over several decades in notoriously compressed articles. In the debates over relativism he is most famous for his paper "On the Very Idea of a Conceptual Scheme" (in Davidson 1984). In this he challenges the intelligibility of the notion of alternative conceptual schemes. His chief philosophical mentor is Quine, yet he develops Quine's work in ways that lead him into direct conflict with his teacher. For example, he abandons Quine's austere behaviourism for an account of mind and language that makes full use of notions of belief and desire. He challenges Quine's reliance on observation as a touchstone of truth, repudiating empiricism as an epistemological position. The notion of truth plays a central explanatory role in his account of meaning, in contrast to Quine's deflationist approach to both of these. Notwithstanding these major differences, Davidson believes that Quine sets up the arena in which the central philosophical debates take place. So he endorses Quine's attack on the two dogmas of empiricism: verificationism and the analytic–synthetic distinction. He holds that his own attack on what he describes as the third dogma of empiricism – scheme–content dualism – is in the spirit of Quine and a logical development of his work. His account of language takes as its point of departure Quine's discussion of radical translation in *Word and Object*. All these various threads feature in Davidson's rejection of relativism, which is what makes his contribution both dialectically sophisticated and frustratingly allusive and difficult to chart.

Davidson denies that one can make sense of the idea of radically alternative conceptual schemes. In so doing he challenges the associated notions of incommensurability and of the dichotomy of conceptual scheme versus interpreted content. He begins his assault by noting that the basic intuition driving many proponents of these views is that of there being various points of view on the world. However, this metaphor only makes sense in the context of there being a basic underlying grid that coordinates the differing points of view. And this underlying grid belies the emphasis on difference. As he says "The trouble is, as so often in philosophy, it is hard to improve intelligibility while retaining the excitement" (1984: 183). Whatever use can be made of any of these notions is either rendered prosaic and unexciting, or else unintelligible. What specific issues does he target and how does he deal with them?

He makes concrete the notion of having a conceptual scheme by assimilating it to the notion of possessing a language. However, it may be the case that speakers of different languages share the same conceptual scheme. So, to accept the idea of having alternative conceptual schemes is to entertain the possibility of there being non-intertranslatable languages – languages that are cut-off from each other or incommensurable. Davidson suggests that a short way of dealing with such a proposal is to say that the evidence that points towards language-hood and the evidence that points towards non-translatability pull in opposing directions. You might recall this as the strategy Quine takes over alternative logics: evidence for deviant logic is always also stronger evidence for mistranslation. Davidson's point is that if what is being discussed is a language, then one can always make sense of the idea of translating it; if not, then it cannot count as a language. While thinking this short option to be true, he thinks it can be given further demonstration. So he distinguishes two possible scenarios in which claims could be made for alternative conceptual schemes: complete failure of translation between two languages and partial failure.

A basic assumption driving Davidson's argument in this context derives from his philosophy of language. This is that one cannot make sense of translation without making use of the attribution of intentional attitudes to speakers: chiefly, beliefs and desires. To translate a speaker's piece of verbal behaviour is simultaneously to ascribe certain beliefs and/or desires to that speaker. Armed with this assumption, he examines the idea of complete untranslatability between languages. Such a picture is often expressed as the world being expressed, or represented by incommensurable systems of concepts. Examples of such systems are often given from the history of scientific development, where the meanings of concepts change to the extent that a new language is being spoken that is untranslatable into the old. Davidson (citing Kuhn as his example) points out that proponents of such views routinely do what they say is impossible: describe the old in terms of the new. But rather than just citing the lack of congruence of practice and doctrine among the conceptual schemers, Davidson proceeds to try to undermine the doctrine itself. The most common way of articulating the idea of alternative conceptual schemes is to present it in terms of a scheme–content dualism. He cites Whorf, Kuhn, Feyerabend and Quine as exemplars of this view. There is some sort of neutral content, which is carved up in different ways by alternative schemes. Differences between such schemes are then explicated as difficulty in translating between them. There are two families of metaphor used in presenting the scheme–content dualism. The first metaphor is that reality (the world, nature) is "organized", "systematized" or "divided up" by conceptual schemes. Now Davidson notes that no sense can be made of the idea of a single object being "organized" and so on. So the very metaphor presupposes some prior form of individuation in operation; that which is organized has some antecedent identity, an identity recognized by those who purport to organize it in different ways. There is a common basic unity underlying the supposed diversity. This cuts against the view that there is no connection between the schemes, or that languages would be non-translatable. The second metaphor involves notions of "fitting", "predicting", "accounting for" and "facing", and applies primarily to some kind of experience (sense-data, sensory promptings, the given). The same objection applies. There must be some antecedent kind of organization to which these terms apply. Davidson's claim is that any language that articulates experiences (such as losing a button or stubbing a toe, having a sensation of warmth or hearing an oboe) individuates them in a common way, such that a language expressing them is translatable into our common languages. Neither of these families of metaphors produces anything yielding the exciting results of alternativeness or non-translatability.

Having dismissed these two metaphors, Davidson redirects his attention to the notion of an alternative conceptual scheme as a language that is true, but untranslatable. However, he holds that the notion of truth in a language is inseparable from the notion of translation. Our best intuition about how the concept of truth is used is captured by Tarski's convention T, and this connects truth closely to meaning. Convention T states that {"Snow is white" is True iff snow is white}, where the latter sentence-in-use yields the truth conditions and hence the meaning of the former sentence, which is mentioned. We can't deploy the notion of truth in isolation from the notion of meaning. Therefore, to suggest that we can entertain the possibility of holding a language to be true but untranslatable is to separate meaning from truth in an illegitimate manner. So there is no joy from that approach for the conceptual schemers.

Given the failure to explain the notion of alternative conceptual schemes by means of complete breakdown of translation, Davidson turns to the possibility of explaining it using partial failure. Perhaps one could make sense of alternative conceptual schemes by reference to a shared common part of the scheme, which then contrasts with the alternative bits. That is, there's a certain amount of shared scheme and then some non-shared schemes that are alternatives to each other. Davidson uses a simple example to discuss this possibility. Think of someone who refers in your presence to a kind of boat you know isn't the boat actually present (the person says "ketch" and you know it's a "yawl"). Either his observational powers are awry or he is using language differently to the way you do. The former situation poses no problems – it is a simple misperception. The latter case, however, could be grounds for defending alternative conceptual schemes; he is using alternative concepts in this area. Davidson indicates that rather than leading to some deep theory of alternative concepts, the example seems much more likely to be a case of malapropism, which can be readily corrected. In conversation we systematically make allowances for such errors and adjust our interpretation accordingly. We interpret him as having beliefs basically similar to our own in the circumstances. Davidson holds that more exotic examples follow the pattern of the simple case; apparently divergent beliefs, or concepts, are assimilated in systematic ways to ours. In interpreting what speakers have to say, charity is a precondition, and not an added extra. That is, we assume that most of what they say is true, and that means assimilating it to what we know to be true. Disagreement then only happens in the context of large-scale agreement. Given a great many common assumptions, one could have a genuine argument about whether a boat is a yawl or a ketch, but not otherwise. So partial lack of translation doesn't offer any hope for defending alternative schemes. As Davidson says, "Given the underlying methodology of interpretation, we could not be in a position to judge that others had concepts or beliefs radically different from our own" (1984: 197).

Davidson rejects both sides of the scheme–content dualism. The notion of raw content is dismissed, but then so also is the notion of a scheme that structures or interprets it. The very idea of a conceptual scheme does not work. Part of the difficulty of interpreting

Davidson's writings is the number of different things going on simultaneously in his work. In rejecting scheme–content dualism he also rejects empiricism, which he believes has to hold to such a dualism. He also defends a coherentist theory of knowledge, holding that there is a presupposition that the great bulk of our beliefs are true. His rejection of incommensurability and relativism is part of this complex picture.

In so far as much of the mileage for claims of alternative conceptions of rationality comes from claims about incommensurability, his case proves quite useful for defenders of a core notion of rationality. However, one might not want to subscribe to other elements of the package that makes up Davidson's position. While rejecting incommensurability, he also rejects ontological relativity and empiricism in epistemology. Towards the end of his paper, he says, "In giving up the dualism of scheme and world, we do not give up the world, but re-establish unmediated touch with the familiar objects whose antics make our sentences and opinions true or false" (1984: 198). Now various significant philosophical doctrines are embedded in this sentence. There's a rejection of empiricism – that sensory input can have any evidential role for the truth of our beliefs. The only thing that impinges on the justification of a belief is another belief. Hence the emphasis in "unmediated". Also, the "familiar objects" keep their identity independent of any process on our part of individuation or socialization, or reference fixing. Davidson's case about translation doesn't touch the position in which there may be alternative but commensurable alternative schemes. One could also challenge the epistemological view offered here. Perhaps there are acceptable ways of defending scheme–content dualism, or else there are ways of defending empiricism that don't commit themselves to such a dualism. One could also disentangle the doctrine of ontological relativism from that of incommensurability. That there are alternative systems of concepts, used for different purposes, needn't entail the same kind of incommensurability envisaged by Davidson. There may be the incommensurability of ends – wanting some concepts to perform different roles – but this isn't the breakdown in communication presented by Davidson.

Arguments have been levelled against Davidson's insistence on translation as the most appropriate way of discussing the issue of alternative conceptual schemes. Granting the claim that the best way of explaining such a notion is to assimilate it to language, it isn't obvious that translatability should be the criterion of language-hood. It makes sense to think that one could recognize that some-thing is a language without necessarily being able to translate it; cryptographers do this all the time. Rescher (1980) has argued that interpretation is a more important notion in this respect. To inter-pret is to explain, paraphrase, use circumlocutions and so on, and not necessarily to translate directly. In making connections between languages there isn't the tight fit of translation, but rather the slippage of interpretation, which admits of degrees. Therefore it makes sense to think of alternative conceptual schemes that are closer to us and those that are further away from us. Rescher uses the example of money. There is no way to directly correlate the value of a Roman Denarius to modern currency, but we know it is money because of its functional role in society. Likewise, we need not directly translate term by term from a different conceptual scheme, but rather understand it to a greater or lesser extent by comparing it to our own social functions.

Rescher's examples still concede a great deal to Davidson's basic point: that we understand functions in society by comparing them to our own. However, what Rescher points out is that differences in conceptual schemes are most importantly not differences such that scheme 1 holds something true while scheme 2 holds that same thing false. Rather, a new scheme introduces possibilities that were not there for the old scheme; it speaks of something not hitherto thought. So it is not the case that Caesar had different views from us on the sub-atomic structure of the metal in his sword. This didn't exist for him; it wasn't part of his universe, whereas it is for us.

Furthermore, Davidson assumes that the interpreter or transla-tor has one conceptual scheme embedded in his or her language (while conceding the corollary that different languages may share the same scheme). However, from the point of view of ontological relativity, there may be various conceptual schemes, understood as systems of categories embedded in the single natural language he or she uses.

So what is left of the idea of incommensurability? Meaning incommensurability has been defused as a major source for relativ-ism by means of the notion of interpretation. One can concede gradations in one's understanding of a different language and culture; they can be understood to a greater or lesser degree, as Kuhn and others have illustrated in their researches. However, as a general thesis that denies the possibility of ever achieving any kind of cognitive contact with others, it lacks credibility. As Davidson said, it is difficult to keep the excitement in the thesis after sorting out what it exactly entails. Knowledge incommensurability can have a limited scope in terms of local conceptions of rationality. This holds that there are different systems of justification, appropriate to different domains and it is inappropriate to apply the standards of one of them to the others. However, crucially, it is possible to argue about them, to challenge the appropriateness of the standards, to supplement them or change them. This is done from the standpoint of the core conception of rationality. So, while we might accept a plurality of local systems, we don't just accept that as an unalterable datum, but argue about it. The mere presence of widespread disagreement between cultures and societies doesn't preclude the possibility of that disagreement being rational and amenable to argumentation, rather than amenable to some other less savoury mode of persuasion or coercion. Value incommensurability is a topic for another book about moral relativism, but it is relevant here as a way of explaining the motivation for ontological relativity. If it is the case that the way we conceptualize reality is shot through with our interests and preoccupations, and if these preoccupations are irreducibly plural, then our ontology will also be pluralistic. Hence, value incommensurability underlies the views expressed in Chapter 3.

At this stage it is time to step back and take an overview of the position now reached, which is the job of Chapter 6.

6 Evaluating relativism

Chapters 2–5 have examined relativism in a number of specific areas of philosophy. In Chapter 2 it was argued that it is incoherent to think of truth as being relative. The argument centred on the claim that the possibility of contradiction was essential to communication and argument. By holding to relative conceptions of truth, one rules out the possibility of contradiction and so endangers communication and argumentation. Because of the significance of contradiction, it furthermore became clear that the limits of logic are established in acknowledging it. One may have alternative systems of logic, but there is a presumption in favour of the dominance of systems holding to the law of non-contradiction. Any calculus that allows contradictions can only be used in a restricted way, and not a universal one. It has to be governed by a higher-level logic that obeys the law of non-contradiction.

Much of what motivates people to accept relativism can be accommodated by ontological relativism, as argued for in Chapter 3. This position attempts to overcome traditional dichotomies such as realism and idealism by rethinking and reconceptualizing the relationship of thought, language and world. The new picture allows for a variety of alternative sets of categories by which the world is mediated to us. None of these is held to be true of the world in itself. The argument goes that that way of thinking about the issues has been superseded.

Relativism features in a variety of ways in contemporary epistemology, as charted in Chapter 4. A new conception of knowledge, which tries to defuse sceptical worries, allows the possibility of accommodating relativistic thinking into key debates such as foundationalism–coherentism and internalism–externalism. The closing section of the chapter suggested a way of thinking about a priori knowledge that allowed the ontological relativism of Chapter 3 and the limited logical relativism of Chapter 2. Chapter 5 held to a core conception of rationality, which is universal. Arguing against localized conceptions of rationality and against claims for incommensurability, four principles of this core conception were articulated. However, unlike Davidson's rejection of incommensurability, this conception of rationality does allow ontological relativism. So the dialectical tension throughout this book has been one of attempting to exploit certain insights promoting relativism, coming from a broad range of disciplines, while simultaneously blocking the kinds of relativism that lead to intellectual nihilism – which many philosophers have correctly identified. However, more can be said about what distinguishes good from bad relativism.

Good and bad relativism

The objectionable form of the position manifests itself most obviously in what can be called "facile" relativism. This is a broad cultural phenomenon in the Western world. It primarily involves belief in the relativity of truth, being generally expressed in the "true for me" idiom. It is usually associated with liberal political views and the belief that to hold to certain things as true absolutely is to revert to a kind of intellectual totalitarianism characteristic of earlier ages. Anecdotal evidence abounds that this view is widespread across the humanities in Western liberal universities. It hits the media in sound-bite references to the postmodern age, a time of irony, or sophisticated jadedness with such superannuated concepts as truth. The diagnosis of the problems underlying this view was presented in Chapter 2. Such relativism has been one of the central targets of Allan Bloom's conservative analysis of modern American universities, in *The Closing of the American Mind* (1987). In that book he characterized the lack of firm convictions and lack of basic intellectual skills in the student community and chronicled what he regarded as the dumbing-down of society in general. The relativism he saw as endemic is, he held, really a form of nihilism. It leads to intellectual corruption, and he charted the paths by which this happens, arguing that various politically correct educational programmes serve students badly by giving them low-grade intellectual fare. He cites various kinds of cultural studies and ethnically oriented educational programmes as examples of this. Much of what Bloom says rings true, and his assault on contemporary facile relativism is quite correct in many of its claims. However, much also rings false, as his response is to return to a mythical society where a highly cultivated class of people with exquisitely cultivated sensibilities supply a cultural elite who are arbiters of truth and taste. It is precisely this kind of cultural chauvinism that lends greatest fuel to the fires of facile relativism. Cultures that are regarded as non-mainstream are judged as having objectively lesser literatures and intellectual power than certain privileged ones represented in the great Western canon. Those excluded from this by reason of gender, ethnicity or social class find the ploy of facile relativism a useful tool against such cultural idolatry. That view is reminiscent of Heidegger's attitude to the Greek and German languages as being somehow "special" or "deep", yielding a greater access to the truths of being than Descartes's French, Berkeley's Hiberno-English or Aquinas's Latin. Heidegger's claim is seen by many as the articulation of a Romantic delusion, rooted in ignoble sentiments that he notoriously never repudiated. So, ironically, patrician attempts such as Bloom's to establish a universal standard have the effect of furthering the impulse to relativism. The criticism of facile relativism is valid, but Bloom's solution is assuredly not, relying as it does on the return to a past that never really was. Indeed, most forms of responding to relativism by appealing to the past seem to ignore the inner dynamic of philosophy. I'll say more about this in the next section.

There are, however, deeper forms of bad relativism that are not as readily dismissible as popular facile relativism: the philosophical forms. In many incarnations, such philosophical relativisms are amorphous and explicitly resist attempts to specify positions or identify arguments and often manifest in areas such as literary theory, cultural theory, gender theory and so on. Many accept a general stance of relativism as given, unquestionable except perhaps by a few reactionaries. But often such a stance is a mixture of the different positions distinguished in this book, lumped together and taken as a package. Such a harnessing together is a problem.

However, there is a general argument that, I believe, identifies the deeper problem with such views. What is deeply problematical about bad relativism is that the views articulated are such as to undermine the very process by which they are articulated. That is, they serve to undermine the process of articulating positions, making arguments and having rational debate. Generally, proponents of these views claim that they challenge monolithic conceptions of position-stating, arguing and rationality. I have argued for core notions of these that must be adhered to. To go against them is to be caught in a dilemma. Either you argue for your new position and so in the very performance of that argument undermine yourself, or else you carry on your idiosyncratic discourse but become isolated from the rest of the intellectual community, particularly from the sciences.

One can generalize the point to say that certain kinds of philosophical theorizing just lose touch with practice and many of these theories advocate radical relativism. Such theorists undermine the intelligibility of the mundane activities that make up most of one's day: dealing with family, colleagues, employers, banks, commerce, and so on. We use non-relativized rationality in these dealings, a rationality undermined by nihilistic theory. It is important to note that this is not a positive argument regimenting common sense to defend a philosophical position – like, for example, the position of Michael Devitt in Chapter 3, arguing that realism supports common sense. Rather it is a negative (perhaps Humean) argument, showing that common-sense mundane activities are incompatible with certain kinds of theorizing.

So what, then, of good relativism? Can any version of the position evade the problems besetting bad relativism? Well, the simple characterization of good relativism is to say it is the kind that doesn't undermine the process of expressing it or arguing about it. Good relativism is underpinned by a methodological absolutism. There is a fixity in our notion of reasoning in general and arguing in general that allows for diversity in results. The diversity appears as alternative sets of categories – alternative concepts that yield alternative ontologies and alternative systems of a priori knowledge. Crucially, rational debate is possible in deciding whether an ontology or conceptual scheme is acceptable or not.

The main position rejected by good relativism is crude reductionism. Reductionism usually gets a bad press, yet it is an essential intellectual process. The very process of thinking about the world is discriminatory: one picks certain features and leaves out others. We generalize, prioritize and make hierarchies; if we didn't our thinking wouldn't amount to much. To reduce some diverse area to its general principles is absolutely basic to all systematic knowledge. Mapping is reductionist; a map that is identical in all respects with that which is mapped is just useless. So reductionism is not just a good thing – it is essential to thought. However, *crude* reductionism is an inappropriate application of this procedure. It leaves out things that are important. It produces a map or an explanation that is deficient in some sense or other, that fails to address important issues. Relativism holds that no single map, no matter how comprehensive, can do justice to the world. We need conceptual schemes that differ from each other to do justice to the richness and diversity of human experience. An issue of terminology may arise here. Because of the problems with bad relativism, some prefer to call this position pluralism. However, because the claim is that ontology, categorization and conceptualization are not absolute, but rather are relative to language, choice, interest and purposes, it seems that relativism is an appropriate title for this position. Once the position itself is clear, the title doesn't matter.

Projects for moderate relativism

The main problem for bad relativism is that it leads to cognitive nihilism. A phenomenon worth noting is that there is a tendency for some on both sides of the debate to assimilate relativism to nihilism. On the one hand there are those who deny secure foundations for truth and knowledge and in so doing espouse a free for all, a Heraclitean free play of signifiers, a sea of shifting identities and no stability of any kind. They accept this conclusion, and consider the possibility of any kind of philosophical attempt to impose fixity on this as misguided and doomed. On the other hand, those who reject this picture as a kind of intellectual suicide see relativism as being inextricably tied to it, and so conflate all kinds of relativism into one kind – bad. However, relativism and nihilism are not linked in this way. If one rejects an absolutist, non-relativistic account of thought, knowledge and reality (let us call that position Platonism, irrespective of whether or not Plato held it), there is not only one other option: nihilism. To use a logical vocabulary, Platonism and nihilism are not contradictories, but contraries. There are mid-points available between them – which is the space that this book has been attempting to map.

An important task, therefore, is to separate good and bad relativism and to explore the ways in which good, non-self-refuting relativism can be articulated. The previous chapters have indicated various ways in which this can be done, but also merely scratched the surface. What avenues of research are open?

Clarifying the relationship of theories of truth to relativism is an important issue. I have argued that truth itself is to be regarded as a universal feature of discourse. However, I also indicated that, depending on the theory of truth one uses, there are implications for relativism in other areas. Giving a clear account of these implications across different theories of truth would be an important task. For example, if one holds to an epistemic account of truth, that truth is something like idealized warranted belief, what curbs does that place on epistemological relativism? If the analyses of truth and knowledge are internally linked, then there is less room to manoeuvre than if they are separate.

The ontological relativism I discussed in Chapter 3 suffers greatly from a lack of worked-out examples. Indeed, this is one of the main objections levelled by opponents of the position. A focussed attempt to develop alternative ontologies in some detail would be very useful. Specifically, what is required is an account of two ontologies that are genuinely alternatives to each other. That means that they cannot be such that they could be concatenated together to form a single complex account of the world. So they are genuine rivals in that they cannot be held simultaneously together. The relativizing move in the ontology is driven by a desire to avoid contradiction and yet to hold on to the properties expressed by the ontologies. The examples used by Putnam and Quine to illustrate their theoretical points are not very convincing, while Strawson's somewhat more meaty examples are not sufficiently worked out.

Given that the different radical positions outlined by Rorty and Stich were rejected, a detailed account of moderate epistemological relativism is required. The work in contextualism in recent years looks like a fruitful resource for this kind of enquiry. Under what local circumstance do we think that someone is justified in holding a belief? What kinds of standard are required, and which ones do we think appropriate for holding a belief? The Cartesian system required that beliefs be indubitable; any possibility of doubt rendered them unjustified. Contextualists, as we have seen, hold that this is too strict – one has to be sensitive to what is appropriate or inappropriate doubt. In the realm of a priori knowledge, there have been a number of significant recent reactions to Quinean scepticism about the a priori. Especially, there has been a renewal of efforts in the rationalist tradition – notably work by Katz, Bonjour and Casullo – attacking Quine and establishing an account of the a priori based on non-sensory intuition. This approach is unsympathetic to relativism about the a priori. To adequately defend such relativism, one needs to address the powerful arguments coming from this group of writers.

I outlined the principles of a universal account of rationality. Clearly, much more needs to be done there. They are appropriately minimal, but what of more detailed applications of them? The principles about evidence, for example, gave no indication as to what counts as evidence. Significant difference may arise as to what this is. Also, I left open the view that different local theories of rationality may be tacked on to the universal theory, agreeing with it but differing from each other. Working through the details of what these might be like would be a significant task. There is also the major task of investigating the connections between rationality and morality. I have studiously avoided any question of moral relativism in the discussion. Yet when discussing rationality, the question of human goods and whether such issues play a role in grounding our notion of rationality begin to emerge. This is something beyond the scope of this book, but clearly requires thought. However, giving a more detailed account of the foundations of the theory of rationality is a requirement for this book. Is it empirical, pragmatic, transcendental or something else? I shall turn to this in the next and final section.

The limits of reason

One of the claims of this book has been that there is a universal account of rationality that all people ought to follow. The central argument for this has been that it is implicit in all our attempts to argue, justify, explain and reason. When we go against one of the four principles we are being irrational. This appears to be a commitment to a very strong form of rationalism: that humans are rational animals. However, at least as far back as Jonathan Swift, there were doubts about this claim. He wryly observed that human beings are animals *capable* of reasoning, but that we are not rational in most of our affairs. Hume also queried the role reason played in our life, holding famously that it was the slave of the passions. Kant circumscribed its limits, arguing that many of the issues that were most philosophically and existentially important to us – the existence of God, the nature of the self, the nature of reality – were not answerable by means of reason; they were beyond its scope. Wittgenstein postulated the mystical, the realm whereof we must keep silent; it can only be shown, not said. Recent psychologists (see Stich 1990) have brought forward significant empirical data showing that fallacies are generally accepted by many people in their regular reasoning, and that we may trade off absolute rational acceptability against other issues, such as limited resources. A quick and dirty solution is often preferable to lengthy and proper method. So where do these considerations leave the adherence to universal principles of rationality?

Well, it seems important to distinguish irrationality from "arationality". Being irrational is contravening the principles of reason. Being arational is not engaging with them – neither obeying nor contravening them. I have presented rationality as being central to our argumentative strategies, to our theorizing about the world and ourselves and to the pursuit of truth. However, these activities are only part of what it is to be human. They are part of our reflective, theoretical attitude to our environment, but there are many other attitudes that we take to the world. We respond emotionally to the world; joy, fear, hope, delight and terror are all part of our emotional repertoire. We respond physically to the world, feeling pain, pleasure, hunger, cold and cramp, for example. We respond capriciously to the world, making jokes, humming, performing rituals of varying kinds and striking poses. There are many other forms of human activity that don't involve argument: dancing, painting, daydreaming, enjoying a good meal and so on. Characterizing these activities as arational is not to call them irrational. Rather it is to circumscribe the role reason plays in our life. We may indeed use reasoning as part of these pursuits (e.g. resolving that I will get lessons in order to play the piano better), but most of these facets of our lives are not supported by argumentation, analysed theoretically or dependent on rational foundations in order to play a full part in our lives. In this sense they are arational – they just don't mesh with reasoning.

This is not to say that they couldn't be the object of rational study: that one couldn't produce a theory of dancing, for example, examining its purposes, modes, history and so on. That study would obey the principles of rationality, but dancing itself neither obeys nor disobeys them – it doesn't connect with them. This is an important distinction, as many who are impelled to argue for alternative conceptions of rationality do so from the desire to show that activities that do not seem to cohere with the standard model are not irrational. But this derives from seeing these as the only two options. It seems that the invaluable lesson of Hume, in particular, was to show that there is much in our make-up that is not governed by reason.

What, then, is the status of the principles of reason articulated in Chapter 5? Given that I have argued for relativity in ontology, and universalism for these principles, is a contradiction not thereby generated? That is, these principles hold good for all times and places, but I have argued that ontology is relative to interest, linguistic apparatus, goals and aims of those producing the ontology. What mode of existence do these principles have? Since they are absolute, don't they constitute an exception to ontological relativity? The principles are arrived at by abstraction, or extrapolation, from our practices. We have practices of reasoning and arguing that we see to be constituted by these principles. That is, when someone deviates from them we no longer think of them as engaging in that practice. The principles don't exist as abstract entities, apart from the practice. They are codifications of a certain kind of practice. In terms of ontology, what exist are beings that perform certain activities that the principles explain. They articulate the nature of that practice. The beings that perform the practice may be described using alternative systems of concepts, yielding ontologies with different kinds of properties (Strawson's examples are of austere scientific properties versus psychological or moral properties). However, the practice of attempting to understand and reason about those properties has a distinctive nature, which is expressed in these principles. The principles are methodological, in the sense that they govern a method, a practice. Whatever theory, or ontology, we deploy in interpreting and understanding reality is put together under the governance of these principles. So a certain kind of practice is regarded as universal: the practice of reasoning and arguing. This doesn't conflict with ontological relativism.

Can these principles change? The answer to this is equivocal – yes and no – because the question is equivocal. In so far as they codify a particular kind of practice that we value and universally deploy, no, they do not change. However, if it came to be the case that we no longer universally valued and deployed that practice, then those principles would not play the role they do, and new principles governing the new practice would be the focus of our attention. So, in that sense, one might say that the principles do change, or new principles replace the old ones. Is this a genuine possibility, that we might supplant our practice of reasoning with a different kind of practice? It is hard to imagine how it could be, yet given the spectacular failures of armchair a priori prohibitions in the history of philosophy, one should be wary about a confident claim in this matter. Could we abandon non-contradiction? It would involve a kind of practice where literal claims that generated disagreement didn't play a role. Perhaps some sort of poetical, metaphorical mode of intellectual exchange would predominate. Indeed, poets, mystics, psychotherapists and mythologists might claim that they indeed value these practices at the moment more than the traditional rational approach. However, what is at stake here is a general universal replacement of the rational method with an alternative – not that there are alternatives that can coexist with rational argumentation, as arational practices. This kind of change seems very unlikely, given the kinds of upheaval in human exchanges this would make (for example the poets, mystics, etc. would have to talk to their car mechanics in this non-factual mode, which does seem to offer comic, if not conceptual, potential). So a general move from the current principles of rationality to a new set is not, in principle, impossible, but in fact seems very unlikely. Unlike a purely a priori argument for the universality of rationality, this isn't closed. It could be shown that what we call rationality has been replaced. But enormous changes in human interaction would have to be in place before claims for this become compelling. Those arguing at present for such changes still do so in a way that obeys the principles (see the discussion of Barnes and Bloor in Chapter 4).

As I said at the outset, attempts to find a middle position will draw opposition from both sides of the dispute. Each side will have a suspicion that too much has been conceded to the other. However, I think the position staked out here, with universalism about truth and rationality allowing relativism in ontology and epistemology, has merit and is a good way to move forwards in the debate. It allows the twin goals of diversity *and* discipline, one of which is excluded in each of the opposing poles of the debate.

Guide to further reading

General
There are a number of good book-length discussions of relativism. Robert Kirk (1999) gives an overview of the problem, defending a realist position and devoting chapters to the discussion of various important individual philosophers, such as Quine, Wittgenstein and Rorty. James F. Harris also takes the approach of discussing individual philosophers in his attack on relativism (1992). Harré and Krausz (1996) take a topic-based approach, including moral relativism. A number of good anthologies are also available. M. Krausz (1989) assembles an impressive group of 21 essays. Together with J. Meiland, Krausz also edited a collection on cognitive and moral relativism (1982). Issues relating to the social sciences, anthropology and rationality are discussed in Hollis and Lukes (1982) and also in Wilson (1970).

Chapter 1: Introduction to relativism
Good general surveys of twentieth-century philosophy that touch on issues about relativism include Passmore (1968, 1985) and Ayer (1982). Susan Haack's article on relativism also touches on recent discussions (1998).

Chapter 2: Truth and logic
Lynch (2001) is an anthology of papers about truth. Discussion of some of the relevant issues can be found in Haack (1978) and

Grayling (1990). On the question of contradiction see Mackie (1964) and Burnyeat (1976a, 1976b, 1990). For artificial language see Carnap (1937) and Tarski (1944), with a discussion in O'Grady (1999). As well as Swoyer (1982), Hacking (1982) and Margolis (1989, 1991), further more detailed discussion of the possibility of relativizing truth can be found in Hales (1997) and Wright (2001). On logical relativity see Haack (1996). A defence of alternative logic can be found in Rescher and Brandom (1979).

Chapter 3: Ontological relativism
Discussions of the general issue of ontological relativism and its relation to the realism–anti-realism debate can be found in Blackburn (1984), Grayling (1990) and Hale & Wright (1997). A short recent statement of Quine's position is found in Quine (1992), with the major discussion in Quine (1960, 1969). Evaluation of Quine can be found in Gibson (1982) and Hookway (1988). Putnam's position can be found in Putnam (1981, 1983). Discussions of Putnam can be found in Heller (1988), Margolis (1994) and Hale and Wright (1997). Critiques of the ontological relativist position can be found in Wolterstorff (1987), Searle (1995) and Devitt (1997).

Chapter 4: Epistemological relativism
Many of the issues discussed in Chapter 4 can be found in Dancy and Sosa (1992). A good discussion of Wittgenstein and scepticism can be found in Kenny (1973: Ch. 11). Quine's views are analysed in Hookway (1988). A number of introductions to epistemology discuss issues arising in "Relativism in contemporary epistemology" (pp. 97–106): for example, Dancy (1985) and Pollock and Cruz (1999). For discussion of Rorty see Brandom (2000), and for discussion of Stich see Sosa and Kim (2000: Pt X). On the a priori see Bonjour (1998) and *Philosophical Studies* 92(1–2), October 1998 – a special issue on the a priori.

Chapter 5: Relativism about rationality
Discussions of rationality in general can be found in Cherniak (1986), Brown (1988), Nozick (1993) and Audi (2001). Alternative

rationalities are defended in varying ways in Whorf (1956), Barnes and Bloor (1982), Milbank (1990) and Code (1995). Further discussions of the Barnes and Bloor position can be found in Hesse (1980). Discussions about the anthropological material can be found in Winch (1958, 1970), Wilson (1970), Skorupski (1976), Hollis and Lukes (1982), Simon (1990) and Hollis (1994). Discussion of Kuhn can be found in Horwich (1993) and Bird (2000). Davidson's work is discussed in LePore (1986), Ramberg (1989) and Evnine (1991).

Bibliography

Albert, D. Z. 1994. *Quantum Mechanics and Experience*. Cambridge, MA: Harvard University Press.

Aristotle 1976. *Ethics*, J. A. K. Thompson (trans.), H. Tredennick (revised with notes and appendices), J. Barnes (introduction and bibliography). Harmondsworth: Penguin.

Aristotle 1998. *The Metaphysics*, Hugh Lawson-Tancred (trans. and ed.). Harmondsworth: Penguin.

Audi, R. 2001. *The Architecture of Reason*. Oxford: Oxford University Press.

Ayer, A. J. 1936. *Language, Truth and Logic*. London: Gollancz.

Ayer, A. J. 1982. *Philosophy in the Twentieth Century*. London: Allen & Unwin.

Barnes, B. & D. Bloor 1982. "Relativism, Rationalism and the Sociology of Knowledge". See Hollis & Lukes (1982), 21–47.

Beattie, J. H. M. 1970. "On Understanding Ritual". See Wilson (1970), 240–68.

Bird, A. 2000. *Thomas Kuhn*. Chesham: Acumen.

Blackburn, S. 1984. *Spreading the Word*. Oxford: Oxford University Press.

Blackburn, S. 1994. "Enchanting Views". In *Reading Putnam*, P. Clark & B. Hale (eds), 12–30. Oxford: Blackwell.

Bloom, A. 1987. *The Closing of the American Mind*. New York: Simon and Schuster.

Boghossian, P. 1997. "Analyticity". In *A Companion to the Philosophy of Language*, B. Hale & C. Wright (eds), 331–68. Oxford: Blackwell.

Bonjour, L. 1998. *In Defence of Pure Reason*. Cambridge: Cambridge University Press.

Brandom, R. 1994. *Making it Explicit*. Cambridge, MA: Harvard University Press.

Brandom, R. (ed.) 2000. *Rorty and his Critics*. Oxford: Blackwell.

Brown, H. I. 1988. *Rationality*. London: Routledge.

Burnyeat, M. 1976a. "Protagoras and Self-Refutation in Later Greek Philosophy", *The Philosophical Review* 85(1): 44–69.

Burnyeat, M. 1976b. "Protagoras and Self-Refutation in Plato's Theaetetus", *The Philosophical Review* 85(2): 172–95.

Burnyeat, M. 1990. "Introduction". In *The Theaetetus of Plato*, M. Burnyeat (ed.), 1–241. Indianapolis: Hackett.

Butchvarov, P. 1998. "The Relativity of *Reallys*". In *The Philosophy of P. F. Strawson*, L. E. Hahn (ed.), 91–105. La Salle, IL: Open Court.

Caputo, J. 1978. *The Mystical Element in Heidegger's Thought*. Athens, OH: Ohio University Press.

Carnap, R. 1937. *The Logical Syntax of Language*. London, Routledge & Kegan Paul.

Carnap, R. 1950. "Empiricism, Semantics and Ontology", *Revue Internationale de Philosophie* 4(11): 20–40.

Carnap, R. 1959. "The Elimination of Metaphysics Through Logical Analysis of Language". In *Logical Positivism*, A. J. Ayer (ed.). Glencoe: Free Press.

Carnap, R. 1967. *The Logical Structure of the World*. Berkeley, CA: University of California Press [originally published 1927].

Casullo, A. (ed.) 1999. *A Priori Knowledge*. Aldershot: Ashgate.

Chatwin, B. 1988. *The Songlines*. London: Picador.

Cherniak, C. 1986. *Minimal Rationality*. Cambridge, MA: MIT Press.

Code, L. 1995. *Rhetorical Spaces: Essays on Gendered Locations*. London: Routledge.

Coffa, A. J. 1976. "Carnap's *Sprachanschauung* c.1932", *Philosophy of Science* 2: 205–41.

Cohen, S. 1999. "Contextualism, Skepticism, and the Structure of Reasons". In *Philosophical Perspectives 13 Epistemology*, J. Tomberlin (ed.), 57–89. Oxford: Blackwell.

Dancy, J. 1985. *Introduction to Contemporary Epistemology*. Oxford: Blackwell.

Dancy, J. & E. Sosa 1992. *A Companion to Epistemology*. Oxford: Blackwell.

Dancy, J. & E. Sosa 2000. *Epistemology: An Anthology*. Oxford: Blackwell.

Danto, A. 1965. *Nietzsche as Philosopher*. New York: Macmillan.

Davidson, D. 1980. *Essays on Actions and Events*. Oxford: Clarendon Press.

Davidson, D. 1984. *Inquiries into Truth and Interpretation*. Oxford: Clarendon Press.

Devitt, M. 1997. *Realism and Truth*, 2nd edn. Princeton, NJ: Princeton University Press.

Dinesen, I. 1937. *Out of Africa*. London: Putnam.

Earman, J. 1993. "Carnap, Kuhn and the Philosophy of Scientific Methodology". See Horwich (1993), 9–36.

Elgin, C. Z. 1997. *Between the Absolute and the Arbitrary*. Ithaca, NY: Cornell University Press.

Ellis, B. 1979. *Rational Belief Systems*. Oxford: Basil Blackwell.

Evans-Pritchard, E. E. 1937. *Witchcraft, Oracles and Magic among the Azande*. Oxford: Clarendon Press.

Evnine, S. 1991. *Donald Davidson*. Cambridge: Polity.

Feyerabend, P. 1987. *Farewell to Reason*. London: Verso.

Friedman, M. 1999. *Reconsidering Logical Positivism*. Cambridge: Cambridge University Press.

Gellner, E. 1959. *Words and Things*. London: Gollancz.

Gettier, E. 1963. "Is Justified True Belief Knowledge?". In *Knowledge and Belief*, A. Phillips Griffiths (ed.), 144–6. Oxford: Oxford University Press, 1967.

Gibson, R. 1982. *The Philosophy of W. V. Quine*. Tampa, FL: University of South Florida Press.

Gibson, R. 1988. *Enlightened Empiricism*. Tampa, FL: University of South Florida Press.

Goldman, A. 1986. *Epistemology and Cognition*. Cambridge, MA: Harvard University Press.

Goodman, N. 1978. *Ways of Worldmaking*. Indianapolis: Hackett.

Goodman, N. 1984. *Of Minds and other Matters*. Cambridge, MA: Harvard University Press.

Grayling, A. 1990. *An Introduction to Philosophical Logic*. London: Duckworth.

Haack, S. 1978. *Philosophy of Logics*. Cambridge: Cambridge University Press.

Haack, S. 1993. *Evidence and Inquiry*. Oxford: Blackwell.

Haack, S. 1996. *Deviant Logic, Fuzzy Logic*, 2nd edn. Chicago, IL: University of Chicago Press.

Haack, S. 1998. *Manifesto of a Passionate Moderate*. Chicago, IL: University of Chicago Press.

Hacking, I. 1982. "Language, Truth and Reason". See Hollis & Lukes (1982), 48–66.

Hale, B. & C. Wright 1997. "Putnam's Model Theoretic Argument". In *A Companion to The Philosophy of Language*, B. Hale & C. Wright (eds), 427–57. Oxford: Blackwell.

Hales, S. 1997. "A Consistent Relativism", *Mind* **106**(421), January: 33–52.

Harré, R. & M. Krausz 1996. *Varieties of Relativism*. Oxford: Blackwell.

Harris, J. 1992. *Against Relativism*. La Salle, IL: Open Court.

Hauptli, B. 1995. *The Reasonableness of Reason*. La Salle, IL: Open Court.

Heller, M. 1988. "Putnam, Reference and Realism". In *Midwest Studies in Philosophy XII: Realism and Antirealism*, P. French, T. Uehling, H. Wettstein (eds.). Minneapolis: University of Minnesota Press.

Heller, M. 1999. "The Proper Role for Contextualism in an Anti-Luck Epistemology". In *Philosophical Perspectives 13: Epistemology*, J. Tomberlin (ed.), 115–29. Oxford: Blackwell.

Hesse, M. 1980. *Revolutions and Reconstructions in the Philosophy of Science*. Brighton: Harvester Press.

Hollis, M. 1970a. "The Limits of Irrationality". See Wilson (1970), 214–20.

Hollis, M. 1970b. "Reason and Ritual". See Wilson (1970), 221–39.

Hollis, M. 1982. "The Social Destruction of Reality". See Hollis & Lukes (1982), 67–86.

Hollis, M. 1994. *The Philosophy of Social Science*. Cambridge: Cambridge University Press.

Hollis, M. & S. Lukes (eds) 1982. *Rationality and Relativism*. Oxford: Blackwell.

Hookway, C. 1988. *Quine*. Cambridge: Polity.

Horton, R. 1970. "African Traditional Thought and Western Science". See Wilson (1970), 131–71.

Horton, R. 1982. "Tradition and Modernity Revisited". See Hollis & Lukes (1982), 201–60.

Horwich, P. 1993. *World Changes: Thomas Kuhn and the Nature of Science*. Cambridge, MA: MIT Press.

Hume, D. 1975. *An Enquiry Concerning Human Understanding*. Oxford: Oxford University Press.

James, W. 1956. *The Will to Believe*. New York: Dover [originally published 1897].

James, W. 1960. *The Varieties of Religious Experience*. Glasgow: Collins [originally published 1901].

James, W. 1981. *Pragmatism*. Indianapolis: Hackett [originally published 1907].

Jarvie, I. C. & J. Agassi 1970. "The Problem of the Rationality of Magic". See Wilson (1970), 172–93.

Katz, J. J. 1998. *Realistic Rationalism*. Cambridge, MA: MIT Press.

Kenny, A. 1973. *Wittgenstein*. Harmondsworth: Penguin.

Kirk, R. 1999. *Relativism and Reality*. London: Routledge.

Kneale, W. & M. Kneale 1962. *The Development of Logic*. Oxford: Oxford University Press.

Krausz, M. (ed.) 1989. *Relativism: Interpretation and Confrontation*. Notre Dame: University of Notre Dame Press.

Krausz, M. & J. Meiland (eds) 1982. *Relativism: Cognitive and Moral*. Notre Dame: University of Notre Dame Press.

Kripke, S. 1980. *Naming and Necessity*. Oxford: Blackwell.

Kuhn, T. S. 1970. *The Structure of Scientific Revolutions*. Chicago, IL: University of Chicago Press.

Kuhn, T. S. 1977. *The Essential Tension*. Chicago, IL: University of Chicago Press.

Kuhn, T. S. 1993. "Afterwords". In *World Changes*, P. Horwich (ed.), 311–41. Cambridge, MA: MIT Press.

Laudan, L. 1990. *Science and Relativism*. Chicago: University of Chicago Press.

Laudan L. 1996. *Beyond Positivism and Relativism*. Boulder, CO: Westview Press.

LePore, E. (ed.) 1986. *Truth and Interpretation*. Oxford: Basil Blackwell.

Lewis, C. I. 1956. *Mind and the World Order*. New York: Dover [originally published 1929].

Lewis, D. 1999. "Putnam's Paradox". In *Papers in Metaphysics and Epistemology*, 56–77. Cambridge: Cambridge University Press.

Lukes, S. 1970. "Some Problems about Rationality". See Wilson (1970), 194–213.

Lukes, S. 1982. "Relativism in its Place". See Hollis & Lukes (1982), 261–305.

Lynch, M. P. 1998. *Truth in Context: An Essay on Pluralism and Objectivity*. Cambridge, MA: MIT Press.

Lynch, M. P. 2001. *The Nature of Truth: Classic and Contemporary Perspectives*. Cambridge, MA: MIT Press.

MacIntyre, A. 1989. "Relativism, Power and Philosophy". In *Relativism: Interpretation and Confrontation*, M. Krausz (ed.), 182–204. Notre Dame: University of Notre Dame Press.

Mackie, J. L. 1964. "Self-Refutation – A Formal Analysis", *Philosophical Quarterly* 14(56), July: 193–203.

Mancosu, P. 1998. *From Brouwer to Hilbert*. Oxford: Oxford University Press.

Margolis, J. 1989. "The Truth about Relativism". See Krausz (1989), 232–55.

Margolis, J. 1991. *The Truth about Relativism*. Oxford: Blackwell.

Margolis, J. 1994. "Comparing Dummett's and Putnam's Realisms", *Philosophical Quarterly* 44(177), October: 519–27.

McDowell, J. 1994. *Mind and World*. Cambridge, MA: Harvard University Press.

Milbank, J. 1990. *Theology and Social Theory: Beyond Secular Reason*.Oxford: Blackwell.

Nozick, R. 1993. *The Nature of Rationality*. Princeton: Princeton University Press.

O'Grady, P. 1999. "Carnap and Two Dogmas of Empiricism", *Philosophy and Phenomenological Research* 59(4), December: 1015–27.

O'Grady, P. 2000. "Anti-Foundationalism and Radical Orthodoxy", *New Blackfriars* 81(950), April: 160–76.

Passmore, J. 1968. *A Hundred Years of Philosophy*. Harmondsworth: Penguin.

Passmore, L. 1985. *Recent Philosophers*. London: Duckworth.

Phillips Griffiths, A. (ed.) 1967. *Knowledge and Belief*. Oxford: Oxford University Press.

Pollock, J. & J. Cruz 1999. *Contemporary Theories of Knowledge*, 2nd edn. Lanham: Rowman and Littlefield.

Priest, G. 1985/86. "Contradiction, Belief and Rationality", *Proceedings of the Aristotelian Society* New Series 86: 99–116.

Putnam, H. 1971. *Philosophy of Logic*. New York: Harper and Row.

Putnam, H. 1981. *Reason, Truth and History*. Cambridge: Cambridge University Press.

Putnam, H. 1983. *Philosophical Papers: Volume 3, Realism and Reason*. Cambridge: Cambridge University Press.

Putnam, H. 1987. *The Many Faces of Realism*. La Salle, IL: Open Court.

Putnam, H. 1990. *Reason with a Human Face*. Cambridge, MA: Harvard University Press.

Putnam, H. 1994. "Sense, Nonsense and the Senses: An Inquiry into the Powers of the Human Mind", *The Journal of Philosophy*, 91(9), September: 445–517.

Putnam, H. 1999. *The Threefold Cord: Mind, Body, and World*. New York: Columbia University Press.

Quine, W. V. 1953. *From A Logical Point of View*. Cambridge, MA: Harvard University Press.

Quine, W. V. 1960. *Word and Object*. Cambridge, MA: MIT Press..

Quine, W. V. 1969. *Ontological Relativity*. Cambridge, MA: Harvard University Press.

Quine, W. V. 1970. *Philosophy of Logic*. Cambridge, MA: Harvard University Press.

Quine, W. V. 1976. *The Ways of Paradox*, rev. edn. Cambridge, MA: Harvard University Press.

Quine, W. V. 1992. *Pursuit of Truth*. Cambridge, MA.: Harvard University Press.

Ramberg, B. 1989. *Donald Davidson's Philosophy of Language*. Oxford: Blackwell.

Rawls, J. 1973. *A Theory of Justice*. Oxford: Oxford University Press.

Rescher, N. 1980. "Conceptual Schemes". In *Midwest Studies in Philosophy*, vol. 5, P. A. French, T. E. Uehling, H. K.Wettstein (eds), 323–45. Minneapolis: University of Minneapolis Press.

Rescher. N. & R. Brandom 1979. *The Logic of Inconsistency*. Oxford: Blackwell.

Rorty, R. 1980. *Philosophy and the Mirror of Nature*. Princeton, NJ: Princeton University Press.

Rorty, R. 1982. *Consequences of Pragmatism*. Minneapolis, MN: University of Minnesota Press.

Rorty, R. 1991. *Objectivity, Relativism and Truth*. Cambridge: Cambridge University Press.

Rorty, R. 1999. *Philosophy and Social Hope*. Harmondsworth: Penguin.

Russell, B. 1967. *The Problems of Philosophy*. Oxford: Oxford University Press [originally published 1912].

Ryle, G. 1954. *Dilemmas*. Cambridge: Cambridge University Press.

Searle, J. 1995. *The Construction of Social Reality*. London: Allen Lane.

Simon, L. 1990. "Rationality and Alien Cultures", *Midwest Studies in Philosophy*, vol. 15, P. A. French, T. E. Uehling, H. K.Wettstein (eds), 15–43. Minneapolis, MN: University of Minnesota Press.

Skorupski, J. 1976. *Symbol and Theory*. Cambridge: Cambridge University Press.

Sokal, A. & J. Bricmont 1998. *Intellectual Impostures*. London: Profile Books.

Sosa, E. 1993. "Putnam's Pragmatic Realism", *The Journal of Philosophy*, 90(12), December: 605–26.

Sosa, E. & Kim J. 2000. *Epistemology: An Anthology*. Oxford: Blackwell.

Sperber, D. 1982. "Apparently Irrational Beliefs". See Hollis & Lukes (1982), 149–80.

Stich, S. 1988. "Reflective Equilibrium, Analytic Epistemology, and the Problem of Cognitive Diversity", *Synthese* 74: 391–413.

Stich, S. 1990. *The Fragmentation of Reason*. Cambridge MA: MIT Press.

Strawson, P. 1984. *Skepticism and Naturalism: Some Varieties*. New York: Columbia University Press.

Swinburne, R. 1981. *Faith and Reason*. Oxford: Clarendon Press.

Swoyer, C. 1982. "True For". In *Relativism: Cognitive and Moral*, M. Krausz & J. Meiland (eds), 84–108. Notre Dame: University of Notre Dame Press.

Tarski, A. 1944. "The Semantic Conception of Truth". In *Philosophy and Phenomenological Research* 4(3): 341–76.

Whorf, B. L. 1956. *Language, Thought and Reality*. Cambridge, MA: MIT Press.

Williams, B. 1978. *Descartes: The Project of Pure Enquiry*. Harmondsworth: Pelican.

Wilson, B. (ed.) 1970. *Rationality*. Oxford: Blackwell.

Wilson, E. O. 1998. *Consilience: The Unity of Knowledge*. London: Little Brown.

Winch, P. 1958. *The Idea of a Social Science and its Relation to Philosophy*. London: Routledge & Kegan Paul.

Winch, P. 1970. "Understanding A Primitive Society". See Wilson (1970), 78–111 [originally published 1964].

Wittgenstein, L. 1953. *Philosophical Investigations*. Oxford: Blackwell.

Wittgenstein, L. 1961. *Tractatus Logico-Philosophicus*. London: Routledge [originally published 1921].

Wittgenstein, L. 1969. *On Certainty*. Oxford: Blackwell.

Wittgenstein, L. 1993. "Remarks on Frazer's Golden Bough". In *Ludwig Wittgenstein, Philosophical Occasions 1912–1951*, J. Klagge & A. Nordmann (eds), 115–55, Indianapolis, IN: Hackett.

Wolterstorff, N. 1987. "Are Concept-Users World Makers?", *Philosophical Perspectives* 1: 233–67.

Wong, D. 1989. "Three Kinds of Incommensurability". In *Relativism: Interpretation and Confrontation*, M. Krausz (ed.), 140–58. Notre Dame: University of Notre Dame Press.

Wright, C. 2001. "On Being in a Quandary: Relativism, Vagueness, Logical Revisionism", *Mind* 110(437), January: 45–98.

Index